THE Thunder FACTORY

Below: An early production RF-84F equipped as a standard reconnaissance aircraft. The wing fences, seen only on the RF-84F, are noteworthy.

THE Thunder FACTORY

An Illustrated History of
The Republic Aviation Corporation

JOSHUA STOFF

Motorbooks International
Publishers & Wholesalers

To Jill – for everything

This edition first published 1990 by Motorbooks International, Publishers and Wholesalers, PO Box 2, Osceola, WI 54020, USA.

First published in 1990 by Arms and Armour Press.

Motorbooks International books are also available at discounts in bulk quantity for industrial or sales-promotional use. For details write to Special Sales Manager at the Publisher's address.

ISBN 0-87938-483-2.

Printed and bound in Great Britain.

Designed and edited by Roger Chesneau; typeset by Ronset Typesetters Ltd, Darwen, Lancashire; camerawork by M&E Reproductions, North Fambridge, Essex. Printed and bound by Courier International, Tiptree, Essex.

ACKNOWLEDGEMENTS
Special thanks are due to Jim Boss and Mario DeMarco, long-time Republic employees, for their proof-reading of the manuscript. All the photographs in this book were formerly in the archives of the Republic Aviation Corporation and were transferred to the Cradle of Aviation Museum on the company's demise in 1987.

Contents

Introduction

THE YEAR 1931 was not the best of times to start a new business enterprise: before the year was out over 28,000 American commercial and industrial firms had failed. Yet this was the year that the colourful Soviet émigré Alexander P. Seversky formed the Seversky Aircraft Corporation on the potato farms of Farmingdale, Long Island, New York – a company that later evolved into the world-renowned Republic Aviation Corporation, subsequently known as Fairchild-Republic. It lasted for 56 turbulent years, and, despite a seemingly endless series of lay-offs and violent management changes, it gave rise to some of the most famous aircraft America has ever produced, including the P-47 Thunderbolt, the fighter-bomber that helped win the air war over Europe during the Second World War.

By 1933 Seversky, along with fellow Soviet émigré Alexander Kartveli, had produced the first aircraft to bear his name, the SEV-3 amphibian, which established a world speed record of 230mph in 1935. Seversky (who was always referred to as 'The Major') and his staff went on to develop other sleek all-metal aircraft for the growing US Air Corps and also achieved several notable overseas sales successes as well; however, Seversky's personality always seemed to antagonize those in power and, perhaps, hurt the company in its early years.

He produced the BT-8 trainer and the classic elliptical-wing P-35 fighter, whose lines clearly showed her as the ancestor of the P-47. Sadly, sales to the Air Corps were never brisk, and 'The Major' and his Board of Directors were at odds over what direction the fledgeling company should take. In the late 1930s the company found itself in a financial crisis, unable to raise money to develop further military aircraft, and while Seversky was on a trip to Britain in 1939 trying to sell

fighters the Board voted him out as President. He was hurt and angry and thereafter had very little to do with the company, although he remained a firm believer in, and promoter of, American air power, writing several notable books on the subject. He died in 1974 at the age of 80.

In 1940, as war clouds began to gather over Europe, the company, now known as Republic, designed a new fighter-bomber for the Air Corps that would, clearly, outperform any other then flying. The brilliant designer Kartveli, who had remained with the firm, came up with the original design for the P-47, and from his ideas grew a vast company of more than 32,000 workers (a high percentage of them women) and an assembly line that produced over 15,000 P-47 Thunderbolts during the Second World War. The P-47, an aircraft which had one of the largest production runs of all time, became a legend, flying more than 500,000 combat missions and damaging or destroying almost 12,000 German aircraft. By 1944 Republic was setting production records, turning out more than twenty P-47s a day. The Thunderbolt, with its long range, was the first American fighter that could provide protective cover for B-17 and B-24 bombers all the way to Germany from bases in Britain; it was also flown by America's leading aces in Europe.

With the war won, and no more need for P-47s, hard times fell on Republic. The management did have the foresight, however, to plan their entry into the civil aircraft market before the war had ended. The XR-12 Rainbow, a four-engined, high-altitude, high-speed reconnaissance aircraft for the Air Corps, was produced in 1945, and at the end of the war Republic attempted to market it as a civil airliner. Both Pan American and American Airlines expressed interest in the project, but its high cost, combined with the postwar

Left: A Republic promotional photograph of test pilot Joe Parker and his P-47 Thunderbolt.

7

glut of ex-military aircraft, precluded its production. The Rainbow still holds the record as the fastest multi-engined, propeller-driven aircraft ever built. Republic also produced the RC-3 Seabee, a well-built amphibian, for the private market, but because production costs rose and postwar sales of new aircraft never materialized for anyone, the project was doomed. Over 1,000 were built, however, and many are still flying. By 1947 both projects had been halted and Republic lost its gamble for civil aviation. Its work force shrank to one-quarter of its peak wartime size.

In 1944 a successful project was initiated at Republic's Farmingdale plant – the beautifully streamlined, jet-powered F-84 Thunderjet, the United States' first 600mph fighter. Large-scale production of the Thunderjet for the newly independent Air Force was soon under way. The F-84 was the first jet fighter equipped for air-to-air refuelling and the first designed to carry atomic weapons; it was also the fighter-bomber 'workhorse' of the Korean War. Produced in several subsequent versions, over 7,000 of these versatile aircraft were manufactured for the US Air Force and

Left: In November 1952 the first production swept-wing F-84F Thunderstreak rolled off Republic's assembly line; the boom on the aircraft's nose was for speed calibration only. This aircraft, like all early F-84Fs, featured a conventional stabilizer and elevator, but it now incorporated a deeper fuselage with an oval intake and a completely redesigned canopy. Lined up in the background are straight-wing F-84s.

Right: An F-105B of the 335th TFS, photographed early in 1959. Note the thin wing and tail surfaces for high speeds, the low-set stabilator, and the ventral fin for increased stability.

foreign air arms until 1953. The Thunderjet was followed by the experimental XF-91 Thunderceptor, America's only rocket powered fighter.

In 1953 came the production of the massive F-105 Thunderchief for the Air Force. In the tradition of Republic aircraft, it was soon setting speed records, and it became the Air Force's standard supersonic multi-mission fighter-bomber. In the 1960s, however, as new ideas about cost-effectiveness began to surface at the Pentagon, the F-105 lost favour. This was due in part to Defense Secretary Robert McNamara's somewhat misguided and almost disastrous desire for an aircraft that both the Air Force and Navy could use – an idea that the services never accepted. Production of the F-105 was halted in 1965 after over 800 had been built, but the aircraft performed with distinction throughout the Vietnam War, first serving as a low-level fighter-bomber (a role for which it was never designed) with mediocre success, but later receiving acclaim as a 'Wild Weasel' SAM-suppression aircraft.

During the same period Republic developed the remarkably advanced XF-103. Designed in the mid-1950s as a high-altitude interceptor, this was an all-titanium, Mach 3–5 aircraft with a unique turbo-ramjet engine. The prototype was well on its way towards completion when the Air Force cancelled the project because of its high cost. Even by today's standards the XF-103 would be considered an exceptional aircraft.

In 1960 Republic spent millions of dollars of its own funds establishing a new research and development (R&D) centre just for the investigation of the fast-growing space programme. Through this initiative Republic won contracts to build space-suits, satellites and rocket engines and to undertake advanced research in future spacecraft. It was a brief but glorious

period of involvement in mankind's 'final frontier'.

By 1965 production of the F-105 had drawn to a close and there was no new aircraft contract to replace it. Employment plummeted to 3,700 and the only work left was building the aft fuselage and tail surfaces for the McDonnell F-4 Phantom fighter. Republic's worst crisis yet had arrived. During that year the company was purchased by the Fairchild Corporation of Maryland, a manufacturer of military aircraft, helicopters and space products, thus, probably, saving it from bankruptcy. Things soon began to improve as Republic won subcontracts for the Boeing 747 and Boeing SST in 1966; a contract to produce a vertical take-off fighter with the Federal Republic of Germany was also won, although, unfortunately, the development of both the US SST and the VTOL fighter was terminated in the late 1960s.

During 1968–69 Republic was involved in an intense competition to build the F-X Air Superiority Fighter for the Air Force. Republic and McDonnell-Douglas were the finalists; Republic lost. In retrospect it appears that geo-political as well as other ephemeral considerations decided who would build the aircraft (which materialized as the F-15). There was no question about the excellence of Republic's design; however, several weeks prior to the award, Grumman, Republic's Long Island neighbour, won the contract to build the F-14. It is very doubtful that the Pentagon would have awarded two such major systems contracts to companies located a mere twelve miles apart, but had Republic won, the company might still be building F-15s today.

After losing the F-X competition, Republic strove to win a new Air Force contract for an advanced close air support aircraft, and in 1972 there was much relief in Farmingdale when the company was awarded the contract to build the A-10 after an intensive 'fly-off' competition: a ten year quest for a new aircraft contract had finally ended. Surprisingly, the Air Force seemed indifferent to the A-10 from the beginning. Although the aircraft is powerful, manoeuvrable and extremely strong, the Air Force traditionally prefers to fly high and fast, not snoop around trees hunting tanks. Air Force officials felt that the A-10 should have been an Army project, but Congress decided otherwise. Production was halted in 1984 after over 700 examples were built, and the A-10 is widely deployed in Europe to this day.

In the early 1980s Republic's management was determined to avoid another lengthy period of lay-offs once the A-10 work was over and began to develop two new aircraft, the SF-340, a turboprop airliner, in collaboration with Saab, and a new jet trainer for the Air Force. Joint production of the SF-340 began in 1982 with sales of more than 400 expected worldwide. The company calculated that aircraft no. 205 would represent the break-even point after all the R&D and start-up money had been expended. Ninety-six examples were built before production was halted in 1987 and the company incurred a major financial loss on the project.

In 1982 Republic also won the contract to build the T-46 advanced jet trainer for the Air Force. The contract for the state-of-the-art trainer was expected to have an eventual value of $1.5 billion, for the production of 650 aircraft until 1992. This was not to be, however. Engineering and manufacturing launch costs on the T-46 escalated, and in 1985 the situation necessitated the addition of $89 million in Fairchild reserve money, in addition to the 1984 reserves of $11 million. Since Fairchild-Republic were working to a fixed-price contract, they were forced to cover all costs above the contract limit. Frequent engineering changes caused the schedule to slip badly and Fairchild-Republic decided to proceed with the long-awaited roll-out of the first 'completed' aircraft to prove their efficiency. In spite of the beauful exterior appearance of the T-46 at the roll-out, Air Force officials present discovered to their horror that the aircraft lacked 1,200 internal components. A livid Air Force Secretary complained to the Secretary of Defense, who in turn ordered a contractor review of the company. Prompted by the missing-parts débâcle, the review found deficiencies in

several of Republic's engineering and manufacturing departments. It marked the end of a working relationship between Republic and the Air Force. In spite of a smoothly proceeding flight test programme in 1986 and 1987, the Air Force decided to cancel the T-46 in the light of recently mandated Federal Budget cuts: with limited funds to work with, Air Force officials preferred to have new fighters and bombers instead of new trainers. It was not a surprising decision. With the termination of both the SF-340 and the T-46 programmes and no new business coming in, Fairchild felt it necessary to wind down operations at the Long Island plant in 1987 and dispose of it entirely in 1988. Because of the contraction of the military aircraft industry and the expected limitations on new programmes, Fairchild could see no near- or long-term opportunities for Republic as a military airframe builder. The remaining 3,500 employees were laid off and Republic's hangar doors were closed for the last time.

Clearly Republic's story is a tale of woe and intrigue. The company had spent most of its existence coping with peaks and valleys of prosperity and cutbacks. But during that half century it produced some outstanding aircraft, over 26,000 in all, that will live in the annals of aviation history forever. Here, then, is its story.

Below: The business end of the A-10. The seven barrels of the GAU-8/A 30mm cannon protrude through the aircraft's nose on the centreline, the nose gear being offset to starboard to accommodate this.

The Seversky Years

ALEXANDER P. SEVERSKY was born into a wealthy family in Tbilisi, Russia, on 7 June 1894. His father was, purportedly, the first Russian to buy a private aircraft, and thus the young Seversky developed an interest in aeronautics from an early age. Alexander graduated from the Imperial Russian Naval Academy in 1914 as a lieutenant. Upon graduation he went on to take post-graduate work at the Russian Military School of Aeronautics in Sebastopol. Here he learned mechanical and aeronautical engineering and upon completion of this schooling in 1915, as the First World War was in progress, he joined the forces as a member of the 2nd Bomber Squadron, Baltic Sea Naval Air Service. On one of his first missions, on 2 July 1915, he took part

in an attack on enemy naval units. He scored a hit on an enemy destroyer, but while attempting a second pass he was struck by anti-aircraft fire.

Seversky nearly made it back to base but, within sight of the airfield, his aircraft crashed into the sea and his remaining bombs exploded, severing his right leg. After his recovery in hospital, Seversky gave an unofficial stunt flying demonstration in front of a group of high-ranking naval officers as he wished to return to active flying duty. His wish was granted and within a year he returned to the Front – as the first one-legged Russian pilot. He rose to the rank of Commander by the end of the war. In 1917 he was appointed Chief of Pursuit Aviation on the Baltic Front,

Right: Major Alexander Seversky, founder of the Seversky Aircraft Corporation in 1931, seen here with his SEV-3 XAR in 1934.

Left: Washington, DC, 1919: Seversky, on the left in a black jacket, and still a Russian naval officer, is a member of a group attempting to sell a small rocket to the US Government. The rocket can be seen lying on the ground.

and he was personally credited with shooting down thirteen enemy aircraft in 57 missions; thus he was also Russia's leading naval ace in the First World War.

Seversky received numerous medals and decorations from the Russian Government and in December 1917 he was appointed Vice-Chairman of the Russian Naval Aviation Commission sent to the United States by the Kerensky Government. However, by the time he arrived in the United States in March 1918, Bolsheviks had ousted Kerensky and the Commission no longer had a purpose. Instead of returning home, several of the officers

remained in America and they developed various schemes to sell things to the US Government in an attempt to remain solvent. Among these was a solid-fuel shore bombardment rocket demonstrated in Washington, DC, in 1919.

Seversky was subsequently employed by the United States Government as a consulting aeronautical engineer and test pilot, and among his first responsibilities was helping to get the SE5 into US production by Curtiss. In 1921 he worked with the Sperry Gyroscope Company of Brooklyn, New York, developing a new type of bomb-sight. There he designed a synchronized, automatic device which served as the basis for the later development of Sperry bomb-sights. The US Government bought the patent rights for this sight for the substantial figure of $50,000.

In 1922 Seversky used his $50,000 to establish the Seversky Aero Corporation. The expressed purpose of this new company was to develop new inventions, and Seversky was President and General Manager. He carried on much research and experimentation in the early years of his company but did not attempt to produce any new aircraft. Some of his inventions involved landing gears of various types which would permit aircraft to alight on land, water, ice or snow. He also worked on new methods of structural design, wing flaps and air-to-air refuelling systems. It was during this time, in 1927, that Seversky became a United States citizen and was commissioned as a Major in the Air Corps Reserve, a title he used proudly thereafter.

Financially, however, the company did poorly, and so in 1931 Seversky was forced to reorganize it with the backing of several

Far left: Fellow Soviet *émigré* Alexander Kartveli, the genius behind Seversky and Republic aircraft from the 1930s through to the 1960s.

investors, principally the financier Paul Moore. The new firm, the Seversky Aircraft Corporation, purchased Alexander's rights and he became President, Engineer, Manager and test pilot. During its first two years the new company did little but experiment as before, but it did begin to develop a radically new type of aircraft. Seversky was joined at this time by Alexander Kartveli, a fellow Soviet *émigré*. Kartveli received his aeronautical engineering training in Paris and came to the United States in 1927 while working on an aborted airliner project for transatlantic flyer Charles Levine. Convinced that all-metal aircraft were the key to aviation's future, Kartveli joined Seversky in 1931 as Vice-President and Chief Engineer. It was Kartveli who was to become the driving force behind most Seversky/Republic aircraft for the next 30 years.

The SEV-3

The year 1931 was not the best of times for starting a new business enterprise in America. During that period 28,285 commercial and industrial firms had failed and countless others had struggled. Added to the effects of the depression was the Billy Mitchell affair which clouded the future of US military aviation. Yet this was the year that the first Seversky aircraft was born.

Both Seversky and Kartveli were convinced that streamlined, all-metal aeroplanes were the key to aviation's advancement, and together they designed and produced the company's first aircraft, the SEV-3 (three-place) – which became the one and only demonstrator to interest potential investors in the company. Having no factory of his own to produce the machine, Seversky contracted the EDO Aircraft Company of College Point, Long Island, New York, to build the aircraft.

The SEV-3 (registration number NX-2106) was a novel, beautifully streamlined amphibian which first flew in April 1933. It was a bronze-coloured, three-seat, all-metal, low-wing monoplane with a new and unusual landing gear consisting of two single-step pontoon floats and two wheels. The wheels retracted into recessed slots in the floats, were supported directly from the wings (not the floats) and were extended from the floats by hydraulic power. When the aircraft was operating from the water, the wheels were retracted into the floats; when operating from land, the wheels were extended and the floats were free to pivot upwards, allowing small auxiliary wheels at the rear of the floats, and the tailwheel, to be in contact with the ground. The SEV-3 also featured all the latest innovations in design and construction which Seversky had developed. These included its

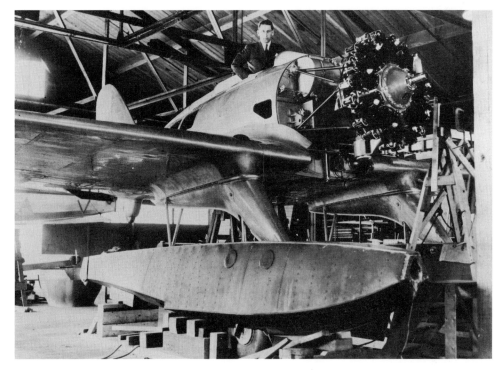

Right: The SEV-3, the first Seversky aircraft, under construction at the EDO aircraft float factory, College Point, Long Island, in 1933. The proud father, Major Seversky, poses in the cockpit.

all-metal, stressed-skin monocoque fuselage and cantilever wing which gave an unusually good weight-to-strength ratio. The one-piece wing was also designed in such a way that its actual structure was used as the container for the gasoline (i.e., it was a 'wet wing'), thus eliminating the necessity of inserting wing tanks. The aircraft was originally powered by an air-cooled Wright R-975 of 420hp, enclosed in a NACA cowling, but the engine was later upgraded to a Wright SR-1820 Cyclone of 710hp. The SEV-3 had a length of 25ft 8in and a wing span of 36ft.

The chief object of most of Seversky's research and development was, however, a long-range pursuit aircraft, of which the SEV-3 was the forerunner. Nonetheless Seversky set several speed records and gathered considerable attention with his SEV-3. On 9 October 1933 he flew the aircraft at 180mph at New York's Roosevelt Field, thus setting a new speed record for amphibians. After the aircraft was re-engined (and re-christened the SEV-3M) on 15 September 1935, Seversky reached 230mph, setting yet another world speed record for amphibians and proving that the SEV-3 was comparable to the best landplanes of the period. This record was among the first of what would become a long series captured by Seversky/Republic aircraft. Needing money, in December 1936 Seversky sold the SEV-3 to Robert Fierro, a Mexican Air Force colonel, who in turn sold it to Gordon Ordaz, the Spanish Ambassador to Mexico. In December 1937 the SEV-3 was shipped to Spain, along with several assorted US aircraft, and it was ultimately destroyed during the Spanish Civil War.

The BT-8

Unlike many other 'speed' aircraft of the period, the SEV-3 incorporated construction and engineering techniques which were easily adaptable to production-line work. Thus in 1934 the SEV-3 was converted into a land-plane by removing the twin floats and installing a fixed undercarriage with large wheel spats. When the Army Air Corps released design requests to the industry for a new basic trainer in 1935, Seversky quickly proposed a military version of the SEV-3, designated by the company the SEV-3XAR. This aircraft was essentially similar to the original design as the Army's proposal did not really require anything new: the specification simply called for a low-wing, all-metal, two-

seat tandem monoplane with a fixed under-carriage. The Army intended that these aircraft be used as basic trainers and designated them BT-8.

Seversky also raised the canopy, installed the Wright R-975, and moved the engine further forward for better balance once the floats were removed. The use of the existing SEV-3XAR as the protoype in the trainer competition gave Seversky the edge over the other competitors: since the basic design problems had already been solved, the Air Corps tended to favour the Seversky design. 'The Major' was also able to demonstrate the SEV-3XAR ahead of schedule. Seversky's main rival in the competition was North American with its NA-16. However, the NA-16 was not ready for trials until 1936, but it was eventually accepted by the Air Corps as the BT-9 and, over the years, was developed into the AT-6 and SNJ trainers of Second World War fame.

Below: Ancestor of all Seversky aircraft – the SEV-3 amphibian. Following its début in 1933 this advanced aircraft set several speed records over the next few years. Here the SEV-3 has had its floats temporarily removed; in this form it had the makings of Seversky's first fighter.

Bottom: By 1935 the SEV-3M had an enlarged canopy, an ADF loop, a Wright R-1820 Cyclone and smaller float rudders. Unfortunately the aircraft was destroyed in the Spanish Civil War.

Right: Fairchild Flying
Field, Farmingdale, Long
Island, about 1928 – the
future home of Seversky/
Republic aircraft. Within
the next two decades
virtually all the potato
farms and pine barrens
surrounding the field
would be replaced by
suburban housing and
shopping centres.

Right: Fairchild Flying
Field, Farmingdale, Long
Island, about 1928 – the
future home of Seversky/
Republic aircraft. Within
the next two decades
virtually all the potato
farms and pine barrens
surrounding the field
would be replaced by
suburban housing and
shopping centres.

In the trials held at Wright Field in 1935, the Seversky outperformed all the other entrants. Thus in mid-1935 Seversky was awarded its first Air Corps contract, for 35 BT-8s (30 trainers plus five spares) at a total value of $878,000. In its final configuration the BT-8 incorporated a 400hp Pratt & Whitney R-985-11 engine. The first production version, designated TBT-8, was delivered to Wright Field in February 1936. All the remaining aircraft were delivered in small batches and put into service by the autumn of 1936.

The BT-8 has the distinction of being the first all-metal, low-wing trainer to be used by the Army Air Corps; it could also be considered the first 'advanced' training aircraft. All the BT-8s were assigned to Randolph Field,

Texas, where they became favourites with instructor and student alike, principally because of their enclosed cockpits, a new feature in Air Corps trainers. The BT-8 was a sturdy aircraft which was considered relatively easy to fly. Its main fault, if there was one, was that it was somewhat underpowered, the addition of a number of military requirements imposing an extra load on the original design which could not be sufficiently compensated for without removing the Air Corps' stipulation that a 400hp engine be used. Major Seversky was clearly aware of this problem, and even before the BT-8 order was completed he had independently developed the SEV-X-BT to prove the basic design could be readily upgraded. By 1938, however, the North

Right: The Seversky BT-8
of 1936 was an advanced
design that made all
previous trainers
obsolete. Its top speed
was 175mph. Here Major
Seversky (front cockpit)
and Kartveli try out the
prototype.

Left, top: A front view of the BT-8 reveals the large flaps, zero-dihedral wing and narrow landing gear. Ground looping was a not uncommon problem.
Left, centre: BT-8s under construction in Farmingdale in 1936. This all-metal aircraft was designed to be built easily on a modern production line.
Left, bottom: The SEV-3M as a landplane, now re-engined with a Wright R-1820 and a three-bladed propeller, about 1936.
Above: Major Seversky with the three SEV-3M-WWs built for Colombia in 1936. These aircraft represented Seversky's first overseas contract.

American BT-9 was selected for use as the Army's new basic trainer and in 1939 all the remaining BT-8s were ordered to be grounded and scrapped. The BT-8 had a wing span of 36ft, a length of 24ft 5in, a top speed of 175mph and a ceiling of 15,000ft.

Meanwhile the original Seversky aircraft was modified again – back to an amphibian – and redesignated SEV-3M, with a Wright R-1820 engine. Because of the previous success of this aircraft, Seversky received an order in August 1935 for three of a similar machine, the SEV-3M-WW, from Colombia, which, with its extensive network of rivers, had a need for amphibious aircraft. This was the first of several foreign sales. At the time Seversky still did not possess his own factory, so the Kirkham Engineering Company of Farmingdale, Long Island, was contracted to build the aircraft. However, before Kirkham had managed to complete one aircraft, and with the other two only at the component stage, all the advance funding was expended and work was stopped. Seversky then took over an empty factory building on the same airfield in Farmingdale and completed the three aircraft as ordered. This move marked the establishment of the Seversky/Republic aircraft factory at Farmingdale, where the company was to remain until its final days in 1987. Seversky completed the three aircraft as ordered and they were then accepted by the Colombian Government with the balance of the contract paid. Fitted with armament and radio equipment, the three SEV-3Ms were used for reconnaissance duties. They had a wing span of 36ft, a length of 25ft 8in, a top speed of 200mph and a ceiling of 22,000ft.

In 1936, to develop further the BT design, Seversky produced the SEV-X-BT, a more powerful derivative of the BT-8. The X-BT was also a more refined design, now with retractable landing gear, a 550hp Pratt & Whitney R-1340 Wasp engine, a Hamilton Standard constant-speed propeller and modified tail surfaces. Major Seversky took the completed aircraft on a tour of the United States and it left a profound impression on all who saw it. However, although the X-BT was intended to develop a better recognition of Seversky designs in general, and trainers in particular, it received little official support from the Government and no further orders were forthcoming.

The P-35

Seversky began to concentrate his efforts on winning a contract for a pursuit aircraft from the Air Corps, which at the time was still equipped with fabric-covered biplanes with a top speed of 180mph. All Army Air Corps fighters were of biplane configuration until 1934, when the first 'modern' aircraft, the Boeing P-26 'Peashooter', entered service. In 1935, therefore, the Air Corps began to search for a replacement for the P-26.

The first attempt at a fighter competition was to be held in June 1935. For this, Seversky offered the SEV-2XP, the second Seversky aircraft to be built. A two-seat fighter, the 2XP was basically the 3XAR fitted with the more powerful Wright GR-1670 engine and a three-bladed propeller. However, fortunately for Seversky, the 2XP made a forced landing and was damaged on its way to Wright Field for the competition. It is extremely doubtful that the fixed-gear 2XP could have defeated the Curtiss Model 75 Hawk that was waiting for it.

Seversky had claimed that the 2XP could attain 280mph but in view of the subsequent performance of the P-35 it would have been lucky to reach 240mph.

With only one competitor ready, the Air Corps postponed the competition until August in order to give Seversky time to rebuild its entrant. Wisely, the company quickly converted the aircraft to a single-seater and installed a rearward-retracting main undercarriage. This new version was designated the SEV-1XP (one-place) and was actually the prototype P-35. It was now powered by an 850hp Wright R-1820-6 Cyclone engine. During the August competition, the revised 1XP had a slight speed advantage over the Curtiss Hawk, although its top speed, 289mph, was just short of the 300mph claimed by Seversky. The Air Corps seemed to favour the 1XP but Curtiss, a long-time Air Corps supplier, complained vehemently that the delay had given Seversky an unfair advantage. Thus the Air Corps put off the final decision yet again, until April 1936. By that time two other competitors had also entered the fray, Consolidated with its PB2A and Vought with its V-141. Both were unsuccessful entrants.

Seversky received a production contract for 77 aircraft on 16 June 1936; of these, 76 became P-35s and the last example became the XP-41. The total value of the contract was $1.7 million at a cost of $34,900 an aircraft. Nevertheless

Below: An SEV-3M-WW, showing its water attitude.
Bottom: Before the BT-8 contract was completed in 1936 Seversky built the X-BT to prove the potential of the design, incorporating several improvements including wing dihedral and a more powerful engine. The Air Corps was not impressed.

Below: The two-seat, fixed-gear Seversky 2XP pursuit aircraft. A most fortuitous accident prevented its appearance at the 1935 Air Corps fighter competition. Bottom: The 2XP was reworked into a single-seat fighter with a retractable undercarriage and was redesignated 1XP. In this form it won the 1936 fighter competition.

Seversky finished with a $70,000 loss for the year. Curtiss however was not to be put off, and in 1937 the company received a larger contract for 210 P-36s at a price of $29,000 an aircraft. As both the P-35 and P-36 went into service at about the same time, Air Corps officers were generally divided into two camps, favouring one side or the other. Major Seversky himself spoke openly with hostility of Curtiss and that company's powerful political connections. He went as far as to tell General Mitchell that 'Curtiss is already trying to pour down the throat of the Air Corps something they don't want. If this happens, it will be a terrific calamity.'

Meanwhile the original 1XP was rebuilt as a racing aircraft (S-1) with the armament removed and various aerodynamic refinements worked in. It was flown by Seversky test pilot Frank Sinclair in the 1937 Bendix Race to fourth place. A sister-ship, the S-2 flown by Frank Fuller and equipped with a 1,000hp R-1830, won the 1937 Bendix Race.

With the purchase of the 77 P-35s in 1936, the Army Air Corps initiated a new generation of fighters. The P-35 was the first American fighter with a retractable landing gear, the first of all-metal construction and the first with an enclosed cockpit. There were a great many changes in equipment and design between the 1XP and the production P-35: a Pratt & Whitney R-1830-9 of 850hp was installed and

Left: The final version of the Seversky 1XP in flight, now with a Pratt & Whitney R-1830 engine. It served, in effect, as the prototype for the P-35 fighter.

Left: The gleaming, classic Seversky P-35 fighter. It represented the pinnacle of American fighter development during aviation's 'Golden Age'. Two 0.30-calibre guns are mounted in the bulges in the cowling, and the landing gear retracted rearwards leaving the wheels exposed.

the tail surfaces were changed to the more familiar P-35 shape. The new model, actually a company-funded P-35 prototype, was designated AP-1 (Advanced Pursuit) and also featured a modified canopy and wheel fairings. For a time the AP-1 had a large nose spinner – which did nothing to help engine cooling.

Seversky spent most of 1937 developing and installing the tools and production machinery necessary to turn out quantities of P-35s, much of this equipment – and the required production techniques – having to be developed from scratch, as is the case with all new aircraft. This was the company's first real experience of the rigid rules governing Army contracts, financial problems began to plague the management and the accounts for the year showed a loss of over $1.2 million.

The production P-35 had a length of 26ft 10in, a wing span of 36ft, a top speed of just over 280mph and a ceiling of 31,000ft. Power was supplied by a Pratt & Whitney R-1830-9 radial air-cooled engine. When the Army first ordered the P-35 the roles for the aircraft were stated as being training, pursuit, search, fighter, attack and bombing. It is important to note that all the aircraft which Seversky produced to this point carried the same design 'stamp': the SEV-3 model's characteristics were carried through to all the others, with the result that they resembled each other closely. The most notable similarity was the highly elliptical wing (somewhat akin to that of the Supermarine Spitfire), which continued through to the P-47 Thunderbolt.

The first production P-35 (36-354) had large, bulging fairings that completely enclosed the

Right: P-35s in production at Farmingdale, 1937.

Far right: The roomy
fuselage interior of the
P-35 could seat two
people.

wheels and no wing dihedral. However, subsequent testing at Wright Field found this configuration to be extremely unstable, the aircraft displaying some dangerous flying characteristics. Stability was improved by adding several degrees of dihedral to the wing and replacing the full wheel fairings with partial fairings. Eventually most (but not all) of the P-35's ills were cured, and Seversky had delivered all 76 P-35s by August 1938, somewhat behind schedule because of the company's inexperience with quantity production. All the P-35s went to the First Pursuit Group at Selfridge Field, Michigan, which consisted of the 17th, 27th and 94th Squadrons. However, by the time deliveries were completed the Curtiss P-36 was already being phased in as the Seversky's replacement.

The performance of the production P-35 was a distinct improvement over that of the Boeing P-26 it was replacing. It could fly faster and higher, and it could take off in a remarkable 400ft. Its range was an outstanding 1,150 miles, whilst its rate of climb was 2,500ft/min. The P-35's cantilever wing was constructed in five sections, with stressed skinning, and incorporated split trailing-edge flaps. The landing gear could be operated electrically or manually and the wheels could rotate freely in the retracted position and be braked.

The P-35 had several important shortcomings. Chief among its weaknesses were a lack of armour and an inadequate armament. By European standards the P-35 was lightly armed, possessing one 0.30- and one 0.50-calibre cowl-mounted machine gun; pro-

vision was also made for carrying up to 300lb of bombs. Other problem areas were the shotgun starter, which often jammed, major engine oil leakage, a faulty gear retraction mechanism and the integral 'wet wing' fuel tanks which leaked constantly and had no self-sealing protection – which would have been absolutely necessary in the Second World War. The P-35 possessed pleasant flight characteristics, however, and, since it still incorporated the basic SEV-3 airframe, its fuselage was quite roomy: often two people were carried in the baggage compartment.

Seterskys for export
Seversky was not slow to appreciate the potential market for military aircraft overseas.

However, spurred by the fear of war, the development of fighter aircraft had proceeded faster in Europe than in the US, so the P-35 was generally inferior in both performance and equipment to its European counterparts. Thus Seversky was not able to obtain much foreign business in 1938 and 1939, being limited to small sales to Russia and Colombia and a politically unwise sale to Japan. Only Sweden showed major interest in the export variant of the P-35. In June 1939 and February 1940 Sweden ordered a total of 120 EP-1 (or EP-106) fighters, and this EP (Export Pursuit) sale allowed Serversky to turn in its first quarterly profit since the company's founding. The EP-1 was, in essence, a somewhat more advanced P-35, and the aircraft were purchased by Sweden to replace ageing Gloster Gladiators. The EP was powered by a 1,050hp Pratt & Whitney R-1830-45 and had a maximum speed of 290mph. The major upgrading was the addition of two machine guns in the wings. As produced, the EP-1 had Swedish guns in the wings but these were replaced by US 0.50-calibre guns after the Air Corps seized the last sixty aircraft; the addition of the two wing-mounted guns, giving a total of four, brought the armament of the P-35 a little closer to modern standards. The appropriation by the US Air Corps of the last sixty EPs in 1940 and their placing into service as P-35As came about as a result of the mounting international tension.

Sweden operated its P-35s as J-9s in *Flygvapnet* F-8. In order to make up for the appropriated P-35s, an equal quantity of

Above: Two EP-106s, export versions of the P-35, just off the assembly line and on their way to Sweden, 1939.

Left: The 2PA, called the 'Convoy Fighter' because of its long range. The aircraft normally carried two machine guns in the nose although it was designed to mount up to four in the cowling plus one in each wing. This was the prototype of the 1939 export version.

Reggiane RE.2000s – an aircraft virtually identical to the P-35 in planform and construction – was purchased. (The RE.2000 is one of those rare clear-cut cases of design piracy in aviation history.) The Swedish EP-1s remained in service as front-line fighters until 1947 and were not retired from service as advanced trainers until 1953.

Meanwhile in 1937 Seversky modified the XBT to accept a more powerful 1,000hp R-1820 engine. This aircraft was then offered to the USAAC and foreign air forces as the 2PA Convoy Fighter, so called because of its long-range capability. It could now carry up to seven machine guns, including a 0.30 for a rear gunner, Seversky preferring a flexible mount in the roomy cockpit to a heavy turret. Fuel tank capacity could be varied between 200 and 350 US gallons depending on the wing span used, with a corresponding effect on range.

In 1938 the USSR became the first country to obtain the 2PA, buying two examples; the size of the Soviet Union implied a need for a long-range fighter. One of the aircraft was fitted with a standard fixed landing gear, the other was an amphibian, and the Soviet Union paid $780,000 for the pair, plus manufacturing rights for the 2PA – one of Seversky's more profitable sales. Later in 1938 Japan purchased twenty two-seat 2PAs (redesignating them A8V-1), intending to use them as long-range, land-based bomber escorts. However, the Japanese found their Severskys to be heavier and less manoeuvrable than many of their existing aircraft and hence the US aircraft proved to be a disappointment. Code-named

'Dick' by the Allies in the Second World War, the A8V-1s were used on the Chinese Front in the reconnaissance role; two were also used by Japanese newspaper companies as fast couriers. Seversky's sale of fighters to Japan, a potential enemy, as late as 1938 did nothing to help its precarious standing with the Army Air Corps.

The P-35 in service

The US P-35s saw brief and inconclusive service with the USAAC during the Second World War. In early 1941 P-35As began to arrive in the Philippines, for a two-year tour, in a belated effort to bolster the islands' defences. They were clearly needed: they were replacing twenty ageing Boeing P-26s. In all, 48 P-35As of the 3rd, 17th and 20th Pursuit Squadrons were in place by May, still equipped with Swedish instrumentation. The next several months saw intensive training on the generally unfamiliar Severskys, with the result that both the airframes and the engines were in need of overhaul by 7 December 1941.

Because of these engine and maintenance problems, the P-35s never had a fair chance against the Japanese. No oxygen was available for high-altitude flying, and 0.50-calibre ammunition was in such short supply that the beleaguered P-35 pilots were forced to rely on their 0.30s. The 34th Pursuit Squadron inherited all the overworked P-35s on 4 December 1941, while other squadrons converted to new P-40Es. By the time of the Japanese attack on Pearl Harbor only eighteen P-35s were available for combat duty. They first encountered Japanese bombers on 8

Left: The land-based version of the 2PA sold to Russia in 1938. It was powered by a Wright Cyclone engine.

Left: The amphibious version of the 2PA sold to Russia.

Left: An impressive line-up of P-35s of the 1st Pursuit Group, 27th Pursuit Squadron, at Selfridge Field, Michigan, in 1938.

December and claimed three victories. However, the lack of an early-warning system brought a swift end to the squadron when a Japanese attack several days later destroyed twelve aircraft and damaged six more. By 1 January only two were airworthy, and these were restricted to reconnaissance missions. The last two flyable P-35s were assembled from wrecks and were flown from the Bataan peninsula in April as the Japanese were approaching. Along with the pilot, two additional pilots rode inside each fuselage, thus fully utilizing the roomy accommodation inherited from the SEV-3 for one last time. In spite of its speed and manoeuvrability, the P-35 was doomed to failure in combat, condemned by its inadequate armour and armament and the absence of self-sealing fuel tanks.

Wisely, the basic P-35 airframe was continually upgraded and developed – specifically by designer Kartveli – through the late 1930s. In 1937 Seversky entered a P-35 (designated NF-1) in the US Navy com-

petition for a new carrier-based fighter to replace the Grumman biplanes then in service. The Navy clearly saw that all-metal monoplanes were the aircraft of the future, and the NF-1 found itself up against the Grumman F4F and Brewster F2A. The NF-1 was the basic P-35 airframe mounting a 950hp Wright R-1820-22 engine. Alterations included the addition of an arrester hook and bomb racks and a larger, bulged windscreen. However, with its top speed of 267mph and its landing speed of 69mph, the Seversky was not considered to be much of an improvement on the Grumman F3Fs then in service. Remarkably, the Brewster F2A won the 1938 Navy competition.

Seversky racers

In an attempt to gather publicity to help win further contracts, Seversky modified several P-35s as racing aircraft. Frank Fuller flew the SEV-S-2 (fitted with a low-drag windshield and canopy) in the 1937 Bendix Race, Seversky test pilot Frank Sinclair flying the Seversky

Below: P-35s of the 27th Squadron at Selfridge. The 27th was allocated the numbers PA 40–69.

Left: Seversky's only attempt to win a naval contract was made with his NF-1 in 1937. However, the aircraft's landing speed (69mph) was considered too high for carrier use. Note the arrester hook.

Left: Frank Fuller's Seversky S-2 racer, a variation of the P-35 fighter. Fuller won the 1937 and 1939 Bendix Trophy speed races flying this aircraft.

Right: Famed aviatrix Jackie Cochran gladly accepted Seversky's offer to fly his aircraft. In 1937 she set a new women's speed record of 293mph in this aircraft, the reworked 1XP; she also won the 1938 Bendix Race with it.

Left: Fuller's sleek S-2 racer on display at a Los Angeles exposition in 1938.

1XP. Fuller won the race, from Burbank in California to Cleveland in Ohio, in 7hr 55min, at an average speed of 258mph; Sinclair came in fourth. Fuller flew the same aircraft in the 1938 Bendix event, although engine trouble reduced his speed, forcing him down to second place, but in the 1939 Race Fuller and the S-2 won again, at an average 282mph.

In 1937, in another publicity stunt, Major Seversky offered noted aviatrix Jacqueline Cochran the chance to fly the Seversky racers. She set several inter-city speed records in the 1XP in 1937, and Seversky offered her a new racer for the 1938 Bendix. The AP-7, powered by a new 1,200hp Pratt & Whitney R-1830 and flown by Cochran to win the 1938 Bendix Race

at an average speed of 250mph, was an attempt to get the maximum performance out of the P-35 design without radical changes. The aircraft was rebuilt for the 1939 Bendix Race, and now featured an inward-retracting undercarriage and a flush-riveted wing; however, problems with the landing gear, and bad weather, forced Cochran to drop out.

In 1937 the Shell Oil Company purchased a Seversky DS as a fast executive aircraft for noted aviator Jimmy Doolittle. The DS was essentially a P-35 with an 850hp Wright R-1820 engine now mounting a propeller spinner. The aircraft was used for publicity purposes and to test the new 100-octane fuel that Shell was developing.

Left: In 1937 the Shell Oil Company purchased a Seversky DS ('Doolittle Special') for its representative Jimmy Doolittle. He used the aircraft for testing aviation fuels and as a fast transport.

Left: The Seversky AP-1 in 1937 at New York's Roosevelt Field. This aircraft was essentially a P-35 demonstrator used for various record-setting publicity stunts.

Left: Major Seversky in his AP-1, holding the trophy for a record 5hr 3min flight from New York's Floyd Bennett Field to Havana on 3 December 1937.

Right: The company's
AP-4 project of 1939 was
essentially identical to
the XP-41, the last P-35
built, but mounted the
turbo-supercharger
which was to make the
P-47 possible.

The commitment to the policy of improving the basic airframe continued. In 1937, in a major effort to clean up the basic P-35 design, Seversky engineers modified a P-35 into the AP-1. A company-owned aircraft used for trials purposes, it sported a new, tight-fitting cowling and a large pointed spinner to reduce drag – an attempt to get inline-engine streamlining on a radial-engined aircraft. The AP-1 was flown to Wright Field for testing prior to the delivery of the first production P-35. The AP-2 featured the flush-retracting landing gear, for greater speed, that was to appear on the XP-41. The proposed AP-3, with a water-cooled Allison V-1710 engine, was abandoned in favour of the AP-4. This was essentially a more powerful AP-2, fitted with a 1,050hp Pratt & Whitney R-1830 SC-2 engine; it was also the

first Seversky to have flush-riveting throughout, self-sealing fuel tanks and a turbo-supercharger, and it was from time to time fitted with a large spinner.

The XP-41

After the delivery of the last P-35 to the Air Corps in 1938, Seversky proposed modifying one of the aircraft into a new, more powerful variant. Designated XP-41, the last P-35 was thus given a new wing centre-section, a fully retractable, inward-hinging landing gear and a mechanical supercharger for high-altitude flying. The XP-41 paralleled the company's AP-4 project. It had a 1,150hp Pratt & Whitney R-1830-19 and a maximum speed of 323mph at 15,000ft. The armament was light – one 0.30- and one 0.50-calibre machine gun – and a

Right: The AP-4, now
with a tight-fitting
cowling and large
spinner which improved
streamlining but
decreased engine
cooling.

Above left: The XP-41, a modification of the last P-35 built. It was equipped with a new wing, a fully retractable landing gear and a supercharger but tests at Wright Field in 1939 failed to show sufficient improvements to warrant its production.
Left: Jackie Cochran and Major Seversky pose by the AP-7 which the former flew to victory in the 1938 Bendix Race.
Above: The Seversky AP-9 was an unsuccessful entrant in the 1939 Air Corps fighter competition. The aircraft featured flush, inward-retracting landing gear but no turbo-supercharger.

lower cockpit canopy was installed in an attempt to reduce drag. Seversky successfully located the supercharger in the belly of the aircraft rather than in the nose like previous supercharged designs where it decreased visibility and made the aircraft nose-heavy. The XP-41 was tested at Wright Field in 1939 but although it retained the P-35's manoeuvrability it did not show enough general improvement to warrant a production contract.

The AP-7 had an inward-retracting undercarriage and was used by Major Seversky in 1938 to set a new transcontinental speed record; it was also successfully flown by Jackie Cochran in the 1938 Bendix Race and, on 6 April 1940, to set a women's speed record of 322mph.

The Seversky AP-9 was another entrant in the 1939 Air Corps fighter competition. Built from the never-completed AP-8, it featured an improved aerofoil and the now standard flush landing gear. It was powered by a Pratt & Whitney R-1830 turning a three-bladed Hamilton Standard propeller but had no supercharger. In spite of these improvements the Air Corps turned down the AP-9 in favour of the Bell XP-39 and the Lockheed XP-38.

Two Seversky designs that were never constructed are also worthy of note. In the mid-1930s, the need for a fast executive transport was perceived and designs

prepared for the Seversky Executive, a luxury, all-metal, low-wing monoplane with an enclosed cabin. The aircraft would have carried from four to six passengers and was proposed in both fixed-gear and amphibious configuration. To a great extent it looked like a larger SEV-3, with a 1,200hp Pratt & Whitney R-1830 engine and designed to cruise at 340mph and at 18,000ft. None was built, although its development might have been possible had Seversky been on a more stable financial footing.

Wanting to diversify out of military aircraft production in a big way, in 1938 Seversky proposed a very ambitious design that was by far the largest ever contemplated by the company. It represented a great advance in size, speed, range and space utilization. Seversky proposed a huge flying boat airliner with a 250ft wing span designed to carry 120 passengers non-stop from New York to London at 300mph. Referred to as the Seversky Super Clipper, it was to feature eight 2,000hp engines driving five propellers. All the passengers were to be carried in luxury accommodation inside the wing, and the aircraft was to be pressurized for operations at 20,000ft. It was to feature twin hulls with retractable pontoons to absorb the shock of landing, and Seversky claimed that the aircraft could easily be converted to an intercontinental bomber carrying ten 2,000lb bombs and with a range of 12,000 miles. The Super Clipper was designed in response to a Pan American proposal for a new transoceanic aircraft but in 1939 the airline decided to order the more conventional Boeing 314. Another advanced design proposed by Seversky was a 'Stratosphere Fighter' with two buried engines driving four propellers.

Corporate reorganization

However, time was beginning to run out for the Seversky Aircraft Corporation. Despite Alexander's constant wooing of the Air Corps with publicity stunts like speed records by experimental fighters, in all the prewar years his promotional schemes had only sold about 140 aircraft of which no more than about 100 had gone to the poverty-stricken Air Corps. Inept management piled up heavy deficits each year, and in 1938 the company was forced to perform financial gymnastics to obtain the funds needed to complete its US Army orders and to continue research and development on new designs which would be needed to obtain future orders – a situation which hardly changed until the company's dying days. By 1938 Seversky was $1 million in the red and was out of favour with the Air Corps because of the delays in P-35 production and the politically unwise sale of 2PAs to the Japanese.

To avoid bankruptcy, a complete reorganization of management and finances was undertaken. Thus, in the middle of 1939, while Alexander Seversky was in England seeking

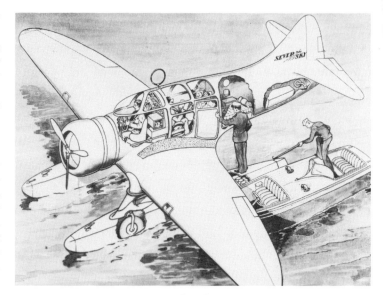

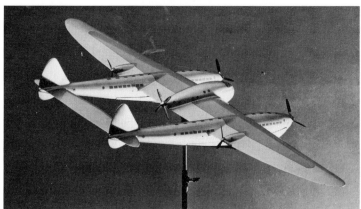

new aircraft orders, the company's Board of Directors, angered at the bleak financial prospects, voted him out as President. Board members charged that too much time and money was going into experimental work, which resulted in fewer quantity orders. Following the issuance of $982,000 of common stock and further major investment by financier Paul Moore, Alexander Seversky was persuaded to accept $80,000 in a cash settlement and W. Wallace Kellett, the head of a Philadelphia autogiro firm, was installed as President. Under Kellett, the company changed its pace. Three weeks after becoming

President, he cut the payroll from 500 to a more manageable 185 while at the same time actively pursuing new aircraft contracts. Then came the fortuitous Swedish export order, and in 1939 the company posted its first profit and soon orders for $10 million worth of business were on its books.

A new name

Following the 1939 reorganization it was decided to change the company's name. Two considerations figured in the choice of name: it should not contain more than eight letters, so that the existing signs on buildings and

trucks could be changed without altering the scale of the lettering or the dimensions of the signs; and the name should be one readily understood in America and in Europe, where the company hoped to develop an increasing export market. The name Republic Aviation Corporation was officially adopted in October 1939.

Relieved of his administrative duties, Alexander Seversky turned to selling his beliefs full-time. He was 'appalled by the routine disregard of air power, especially long-range strategic force, and thus he chose to address himself directly to the American people, above the heads of the military hierarchy in Washington. He wrote a best-selling book, *Victory Through Air Power*, in large part a chronicle of War Department blunders

Below: Varied fuselage markings represented a clear sign of the sudden and unexpected change from Seversky to Republic. Here is Major Seversky in the AP-7, with 'Seversky' on the fuselage.

Left: An AT-12 (ex-2PA) photographed over Long Island.

and military short-sightedness. Its message, however, was one of hope. Seversky's basic convictions, set down prior to America's entry into the Second World War and repeated many times, were:*

1. The rapid expansion of the range and striking power of military aviation makes it certain that the United States will be as exposed to destruction from the air, within a predictable period, as are the British Isles today.
2. Those who deny the practical possibility of a direct aerial attack on America are lulling the American people into an utterly false sense of safety which may prove as disastrous to us as the 'Maginot Line' proved to France.
3. To meet this threat to the existence and independence of our country we must begin immediately to prepare for the specific kind of war conditioned by the advent of air power. That can mean only an interhemispheric war direct across oceans, with air power fighting not over this or that locality, but by longitude and latitude anywhere in the uninterrupted 'air ocean'.
4. Despite immediate shortcomings, there is no excuse for a defeatist approach to the problem. On the contrary, America has all the pre-requisites for victory in the race for domination of the skies. It has all that is required to make it the dominant air-power nation, even as England in its prime was the dominant sea-power nation of the world.

The pressing immediate need is for a national

Below: The AP-7 (with the AP-9 wing), now with 'Republic' hand-lettered in gothic script by Cochran's personal mechanic, German émigré Erwin Hoenes.

awakening to the threat implicit in air power – and to the urgency of preparing not merely to meet it but to take the offensive initiative. Autonomous and specialized organization for air power, freed from the restraints and enertia of long-established army and naval organizations, is almost axiomatic. It will follow, I believe, just as soon as the American people break through their present lethargy.

By 1947 *Fortune Magazine* could report that 'as an author, Seversky had far more influence on US aviation than he ever had as a planemaker.'

The first aircraft sold under the Republic name, although still a P-35 derivative, was the AT-12 Guardsman. A two-seat export fighter ('convoy fighter'), the AT-12 was originally sold to Sweden as the long-range 2PA fighter-bomber. Sweden purchased 52 2PAs in 1939, though all but two of these were seized by the US War Department for the Air Corps in 1940. However, the Air Corps had no real need for Republic AT-12s, so they were used as advanced trainers and fast personnel transports. Virtually all were phased out and scrapped during the course of the Second World War.

---

*Seversky, Alexander. *Victory Through Air Power*. Simon & Schuster (New York, 1941)

Republic at War

ALTHOUGH THE AIR CORPS was not interested in the P-41, it *was* interested in its sister-aircraft, the AP-4. Whereas the geared supercharger on the XP-41 had its limitations, the turbo-supercharger on the AP-4 offered much better possibilities for improved performance, employing as it did engine exhaust gases to work the air compressor, to convert thin, high-altitude air to a density equal to that at sea level and forcing it into the engine, thereby allowing the aircraft to fly higher and faster in the thin air because low-altitude power could be produced. The bulky turbo-supercharger was located in the aircraft's lower fuselage, near the centre of gravity, with ducts to an intake in the nose and reverse ducts back to the engine, the exhaust gases being blown out under the rear fuselage. Tested at the same time as the XP-41, the AP-4 flew higher (up to 38,000ft) and faster (350mph).

The P-43 Lancer
In March 1939 Republic received an order for thirteen service AP-4 trials aircraft, known as YP-43s. However, at the time, the Air Corps

Below left: The proposed Republic AP-12 Rocket, the Allison-powered ancestor of the P-47. Bottom left: The AP-12 design clearly represented the ideal streamlined form as sought by Kartveli. The buried Allison engine would have driven two contra-rotating propellers.

Right: The P-43 Lancer was the immediate forerunner of the P-47 but it suffered from inadequate power, armament and armour. Republic's line was 'kept rolling' only to ease the transition to the P-47.

Below: P-43s in operational service at Selfridge Field, Michigan, in 1941. None saw US service during the Second World War.

were investigating a number of promising fighter designs and thus did not commit themselves to large-scale P-43 production; furthermore, at the time the YP-43s were ordered, the Corps were buying Curtiss P-40s in quantity. Recognizing that the company could be about to face mass-production problems on an unprecedented scale, Republic's management resolved to search for an acknowledged aircraft production expert who could assume the full responsibility for this aspect of the company's interest. In April 1941, just as the first part of the P-43 contract was

being completed, the company was able to work out an arrangement whereby one of the nation's outstanding businessmen, Ralph Damon, Vice-President of American Airlines and formerly President of Curtiss, assumed the Presidency of Republic, Mr Kellett becoming Chairman of the Board of Directors.

The P-43, now named Lancer, incorporated the best features of the AP-4 and the XP-41. The aircraft was originally developed with a close-fitting cowling blending into a huge pointed spinner in an attempt to streamline the big air-cooled radial engine (1,200hp Pratt

& Whitney R-1830) and give it more of the profile of a liquid cooled engine; however this led to problems of overheating and was soon replaced by a conventional cowling. Even with the limited 1,200hp available, the YP-43 was faster than the P-40 and its top speed matched that of the Spitfire. All thirteen YP-43s were delivered by April 1941, by which time, however, it was obvious that the design was outdated by European fighters, the only advantages being its 1,000-mile range and its ability to develop full horsepower at 23,000ft.

The P-44

On 13 September 1939 the Air Corps placed an order with Republic for 80 AP-4Js, designated P-44-1 Warrior and equipped with a 1,400hp Pratt & Whitney R-2180. Apart from a somewhat cleaned-up airframe, the P-44 differed little visually from the P-43, but its more powerful engine would now give it a top speed of 386mph. The aircraft was also to be equipped with eight 0.50-calibre wing- and nose-mounted Browning machine guns, giving it the heaviest armament of any fighter of the period.

Fears of soon being drawn into the war caused the Air Corps to dispense with the prototype stage to hasten production, but just as construction was set to begin on the P-44-1 Kartveli designed an even more promising version, the AP-4L or P-44-2, powered by a 2,000hp Pratt & Whitney R-2800-7 which would increase the Warrior's maximum speed to 406mph. On 19 July 1940 the Air Corps ordered 225 P-44-2s 'straight off the drawing board' and in September 1940 this order was increased to a total of 827. The P-44-2 would not only be equipped with the turbo-supercharger but also would have extra built-in fuel tanks, making it the longest-range fighter of the period; however, it would be equipped with neither armour nor self-sealing fuel tanks because of the limitations of the wing and fuselage structure. Later in 1940 Republic proposed a rather bizarre version of the P-44 – a biplane version in which the upper wing, attached to the forward fuselage, would serve as an expendable additional fuel tank. The tank could be jettisoned if combat were imminent, or, when empty, would keep the entire aircraft afloat if the pilot were forced to ditch. Nothing ever came of the proposal.

By mid-1940 it became clear from combat reports received from Europe that the P-44 design would be outdated by the time it reached production status, and so Kartveli began work on a new, more advanced design which was eventually to become the famous P-47 Thunderbolt. In September 1940 the P-47 design was approved and at the same time all P-44 orders were cancelled. Thus, all at once, Republic was scrambling to define the XP-47, design and build the XP-44, deliver thirteen YP-43s and export 120 EP-1s to Sweden.

Right: Someone at Republic came up with a bizarre concept for a biplane version of the P-44. The top wing, which would serve as a long-range fuel tank, was jettisonable for increased speed if the aircraft were attacked.

Left: Six months after the P-43 was ordered the P-44 Warrior contract was placed. However, Kartveli wisely shelved the new aircraft when he realized that it would not possess all the characteristics the Air Corps was looking for. Its lines clearly show it to be a very close relative to the P-47.

Above: The biplane P-44's top wing could also keep the aircraft afloat in the event of ditching.

the Second World War was looming. For Republic, as for others, the floodgates were suddenly open.

The initial batch of 54 P-43s were powered by 1,200hp Pratt & Whitney R-1830-55 engines with turbo-supercharging. They possessed a top speed of 351mph and were armed with two 0.50-calibre machine guns in the nose and one 0.30-calibre gun in each wing. Later P-43s were equipped with R-1830-47 or -57 engines, which increased the top speed to 356mph. In all, 272 P-43 Lancers were delivered to the Air Corps before America's entry into the war, the last being produced in September 1941. As they were considered unfit for front-line combat, most were converted for use in the photo-reconnaissance role and designated P-43B and P-43C. No Lancers in American service were used in combat, although the Chinese Air Force obtained 108 aircraft from the Air Corps and these were employed in the desperate fight against the Japanese. The P-43 had a wing span of 36ft, a length of 28ft 6in and an empty weight of 5,730lb.

The P-47 conceived

Seversky/Republic's chief engineer, Alexander Kartveli, concentrated on the single-engined, single-seat pursuit aircraft and had incorporated in his designs air-cooled radials of the highest power possible, supercharging, streamlining wherever practicable and the adoption of design and construction methods leading to the best possible performance. As a result of this effort, in 1941 Republic became the first company to deliver to the Air Corps a fighter powered by a single 2,000hp engine. This was the famous P-47 Thunderbolt – although it started life as something very different.

In 1939 most American aircraft manufacturers were turning to the new V12 Allison liquid-cooled engine to power their new fighters as this unit appeared to offer the most power with the least frontal area, thus permitting greater streamlining than with a large radial engine. Republic could not overlook the potential offered by the new Allison and on 1 August 1939 proposed the development of a completely new lightweight fighter similar in general characteristics to European fighters. Republic's AP-10 had a gross weight of only 4,900lb and would be powered by the 1,150hp Allison V-1710-39; its armament was to consist of but two 0.50-calibre machine guns. In essence Kartveli

Originally, there were no plans to produce Lancers beyond the first batch since the P-44 seemed clearly superior. However, once the P-44 was cancelled as inadequate, the Air Corps was forced to await completion of the new fighter, the XP-47. In view of the delay before P-47s would be flying, the Air Corps felt it would be best to keep the production lines at Republic open and active with an already developed aircraft – the P-43; furthermore, the Pratt & Whitney R-2800 engines for the P-47 were not yet available. Therefore the Army ordered the P-44s under construction to be completed as P-43s: even though it was considered second-rate, the P-43 was placed into production as a stop-gap – to maintain readiness and continuity until P-47s could take shape. The P-47 was ordered 'off the drawing board', before the prototype had flown: Republic no longer had to compete for new contracts as the US was desperate for first-rate aircraft – American involvement in

designed the smallest fighter that could be built around the Allison engine.

Insufficient firepower and a high wing loading led to the proposal in this form being rejected but the basic design warranted further investigation. An enlarged version, with two 0.30-calibre guns in each wing and two 0.50-calibre guns in the nose and a gross weight of some 6150lb, was soon ordered as the XP-47 in November 1939; a second example, stripped of combat equipment, was ordered as the XP-47A in January 1940 in order to flight-test the design ahead of the combat-equipped XP-47. The estimated performance of the XP-47 was 415mph at 15,000ft. It was to have a wing span of 30ft and a length of 27ft 6in, whilst the empty weight would have been 4,900lb – a remarkable figure compared to the 8,633lb of the P-51 Mustang. The Allison engine would have turned a 10ft-diameter constant-speed Curtiss propeller. Republic also proposed a similar but more advanced version, the AP-12 Rocket, but this six-gun fighter (four in the nose, one in each wing), which featured a buried Allison engine driving two contra-rotating propellers, was not developed further.

Before construction of the XP-47 could begin, combat reports from Europe indicated that the lightweight fighter design would be deficient, and in May 1940 the Air Corps called a meeting of manufacturers at Wright Field in order to discuss the entire fighter programme and to spell out the requirements for the kind of aircraft it wanted. Essentially the Corps wanted a new fighter, bomber escort and light bomber all in one airframe, with self-sealing fuel tanks, armour plating and a speed of 400mph. It also had to be a high-altitude, long-range aircraft that would outgun and outfight anything the enemy could put up against it. Concerned about problems with the Allison engine, the Corps also wanted to expedite the development of the aircraft using the new air-cooled R-2800 engine. Kartveli listened to these requirements and, as they were clearly

Left: The original full-scale mock-up of the XP-47A. Although a P-47, it bears little resemblance to the Thunderbolt. This was essentially the smallest, lightest fighter that could be built around the Allison engine but the design was scrapped because of inadequacies in performance, armour and armament.
Below: The original XP-47B Thunderbolt – the only prototype built. Essentially this was a larger, heavier P-43 with a more powerful engine, more armour, a better armament and self-sealing fuel tanks. Kartveli stayed with the proven Republic aerofoil and elliptical wing but after the third P-47 the side-opening door was eliminated. Note the absence of a paved runway at Republic's airfield.

beyond the capabilities of the P-44 or XP-47, was asked to reconsider earlier designs. On the train on the way back from Wright Field, Kartveli sketched on the back of an envelope an all-new aircraft that would not only meet the Air Corps specifications but also have more speed, power and range and a greater load-carrying capability than any other fighter. Thus was born the famous P-47 Thunderbolt.

Kartveli, foreseeing the demise of the XP-47, developed a brand new airframe built around the 2,000hp Pratt & Whitney R-2800, the XP-47 being far too small to mount such a massive powerplant. Designated XP-47B, it had a proposed top speed of just over 400mph at 25,000ft and would mount eight 0.50-calibre machine guns. Its total weight would be 11,500lb – about twice that of the original XP-47 – yet its high-altitude performance and armament would better those of any other US fighter then under development. Republic submitted its plans in June 1940.

In September 1940, impressed with these statistics, the Air Corps issued a huge $56 million dollar contract to Republic for 171 P-

47Bs and 602 P-47Cs – before the first one had flown. This was, to date, the largest single order placed by the Air Corps for fighter aircraft. At the same time all work on the XP-47 and XP-47A was terminated, the one completed full-scale wind-tunnel model being handed over to Langley Field for testing.

Although appearing to be an enlarged version of the P-43, the new aircraft was unique in many respects. The supercharging system was the heart of the P-47 and it created many problems during the design stage. In order for the aircraft to attain 400mph the importance of a smooth flow of air between the supercharger and the engine was the most serious design consideration. Consequently the supercharging system of the P-47 was designed first, in order to obtain the most efficient and least interrupted airflow, and the rest of the aircraft was designed around it. The supercharger was placed in the fuselage aft of the pilot, with exhaust gases piped back to the turbine and expelled at the rear, and ducted air was returned to the engine under pressure. Despite the fact that the supercharger was in

the tail and the engine in the nose, the system proved quite successful.

The power of the R-2800 engine was too much for the three-bladed propeller of the P-43, so the P-47 became the first US fighter to mount a massive 12ft-diameter four-bladed, controllable-pitch propeller, taking full advantage of the power of the engine. However, in order to mount the landing gear in the wing as planned, have room for eight machine guns and still provide the needed ground clearance for the propeller, a novel solution was called for. A full-length undercarriage would not fit in the wing, so the designers developed a telescoping strut that lengthened the gear 9in when it was lowered. Unlike earlier Severskys, the XP-47B contained no fuel in the wings, a total of over 300 US gallons being carried in two internal tanks forward of and below the cockpit. There was one other unusual feature of the XP-47B. In contrast to the earlier Farmingdale designs, and later P-47s which possessed sliding canopies, the XP-47B canopy opened to the side, much like a car door, although because of the difficulty of opening it in flight it was deleted on all subsequent models.

The autumn of 1940 was frantic for Republic as well as for the world in general. By the end of the year the company was employing 2,600 people, compared with just 176 a year before, and the factory had expanded greatly in order to meet the contract for 773 aircraft; and within a year the company had risen to the point where it was second only to the much older Curtiss Corporation as the largest supplier of pursuit aircraft to the Army Air Forces.* By this time Republic was ready to assume its role in the growth of American air power and the attainment of victory in a global conflict. In early 1941 C. Hart Miller, Republic's Director of Military Contracts, came up with a name for the new fighter – the Thunderbolt.

First trials

By the spring of 1941 the first Thunderbolt was ready to fly. On 6 May Republic test pilot Lowery Brabham taxied the new machine out along the flight line as several hundred Republic employees and executives watched. The roar of the 2,000hp engine drowned out all else – except the knowledge that here was the heaviest single-engined fighter ever built in the United States. It had a wingspan of 40ft 9in and a weight of over 13,000lb, and it had to climb to 40,000ft (the first 15,000ft in six

minutes) with a battery of eight 0.50-calibre machine guns and munitions – a heavier load of armament than any other fighter could carry at that time; moreover, it had to afford the pilot protection from attack in all directions with its heavy armour plate and still give him enough speed and manoeuvrability to fight off any known enemy.

After a surprisingly short take-off run, Brabham flew the P-47 over the field in a series of manoeuvres and passes, then headed for the nearby military air base at Mitchel Field: Republic's Farmingdale runways, unpaved until 1942, were muddy from the spring rains whereas Mitchel had longer, paved runways. Upon landing, Brabham taxied up to waiting company officials and exclaimed, 'What a ship! Boy – we've hit the jackpot!' The one problem experienced during the flight occurred when the cockpit filled with smoke because of oil residue burning in the ducts leading to the supercharger.

On their own, Republic's engineers had considerably increased the P-47's load factors beyond those required by the Air Corps, a decision which accounted for the receptiveness of the basic design to modifications which increased the gross weight of the aircraft from the original 13,000lb to better than 20,000lb as successive models were produced. In spite of increased fuel loads, more armament and the addition of bombs and rockets, the P-47 pushed the limits of maximum operating altitudes further into the sub-stratosphere and at the same time established ranges never before believed possible for a fighter.

Nearly two years of testing and refining were required before the Thunderbolt was ready for combat. On 7 December 1941 Republic employees, like the rest of the world, listened in disbelief to the news of the Japanese attack on Pearl Harbor. Within a week, the plant was on three shifts a day and the employees had chipped in to donate a new Thunderbolt to the Government. All the work carried out on this aircraft, which was called 'Lucky Seven', was done so without pay. In early 1942 the XP-47B flew at 412mph, faster than any US or British fighter and at much higher altitude. However, in August 1942 the original XP-47B

---

*The US Army Corps was absorbed into the new US Army Air Forces (USAAF) in June 1941 and the name was discontinued in March 1942.

Above: The beautiful elliptical wing of the P-47 can be traced directly back to the SEV-3 of ten years earlier. Note how the canopy blends back into a dorsal spine.

crashed into the Long Island Sound following the loss of elevator control; the test pilot bailed out successfully.

At high altitude the XP-47B proved to be susceptible to aileron 'snatch', control loads on the ailerons and rudder becoming excessive; furthermore, the sideways-hinging canopy was difficult to open in an emergency. Cures were found for all of these problems, but the P-47's estimated date for entry into combat in 1942 slipped considerably – despite an accelerated flight-test program.

Production P-47s had a semi-monocoque, all-metal fuselage of stressed-skin construction composed of transverse bulkheads and longitudinal stringers. The cockpit blended into the tail via a 'razorback' spine. The engine was covered by a NACA design cowling. A 205 US gallon main fuel tank was sited forward of and below the cockpit and a 100 US gallon auxiliary tank was installed aft of the rear wing support bulkhead. The wing was a full cantilever type incorporating two main spars, supporting the attachment of wing to fuselage, and three secondary spars. Flush-riveted, stressed-skin surfaces were reinforced by extruded angle stringers. Gun bays were situated outboard of the landing gear wells and a staggered arrangement for the machine guns allowed ammunition to be fed in directly via troughs arranged side by side in the outer wing panels. The tail empennage was also of full cantilever structure. Fin and horizontal stabilizer were bolted together and, in turn, bolted to the rear fuselage. On the XP-47B and P-47B's empennage, the control surfaces were fabric covered; later production P-47 surfaces were aluminium-skinned.

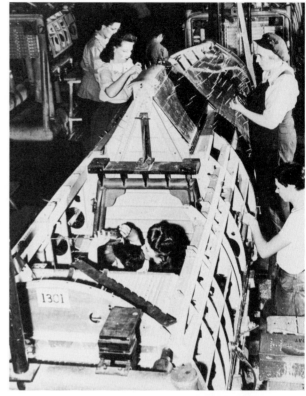

Far left: The final
cowling attachment for a
P-47D.
Left: A high percentage
of Republic's wartime
employees were women.
Here the skin goes on to
the spine of a P-47D.

Far left: Women were
involved in all phases of
P-47 construction. Here a
cowling is riveted.
Left: P-47 tail sections
were assembled
vertically and then
attached to the aircraft.

Thunderbolts into service

Almost a year after the XP-47B first flew, in
March 1942, the first production P-47B rolled
off Republic's assembly line. By midsummer a
production rate of 50 a month was anticipated.
Outwardly the P-47B was identical to the XP-
47B with the exception of a redesigned sliding
canopy and a repositioned aerial mast;
inwardly the major change was the use of a
production R-2800-21 engine driving a 12ft 2in
Curtiss Electric propeller. Armament
remained as eight 0.50-calibre machine guns,
and metal-covered ailerons were fitted. Wing
span was 40ft 9in, length 35ft and service
ceiling 42,000ft. The total weight reached
13,356lb, 650lb heavier than planned, but top
speed rose to 429mph. At low-level the P-47B
proved sluggish, but at high altitude, above
20,000ft, it proved nimble and swift. The one
weakness of these early P-47s concerned their
climb rate, which it was adequate but not
exceptional. In a dive, it was quickly learned
that the P-47 built up speed alarmingly, and
this often resulted in mangled rudders and
crashed aircraft. Thus in August 1942 a
limitation order of 300mph was placed on the
aircraft as well as a prohibition on aerobatics
and violent manoeuvres. When in terminal
velocity dives (at about 500mph) it appeared
that the P-47 encountered the compressibility
factor, of which little was known at the time. At
such speeds the air exerted pressures which
destroyed fabric-covered control surfaces.
Thus it was that by September 1942 Republic
had developed a new aluminium-skinned
rudder and reinforced fin which eliminated
the problem of tail 'flutter'.

In all, 171 P-47Bs were built. The aircraft's
short range of 800 miles and the lack of an
external fuel tank rendered it inadequate for
the long-range escort role, and all P-47Bs had
a 'R' prefix added to their designation in 1943,
placing the aircraft in the 'restricted' category
which meant that they could only be used for
pilot training. The first unit to receive the P-47
was the 56th Fighter Group, based in Bridge-
port in Connecticut, Bendix in New Jersey and
Farmingdale, Long Island. Since the 56th was
already located on Republic's doorstep it was
the ideal unit to put the Thunderbolt through
an operational evaluation. Most of the flight
training was conducted at Bradley Field,
Connecticut, as the P-47 required nearly half a
mile to become airborne and Bradley's
runway was a mile long. At first most pursuit
pilots were intimidated by the size, weight

and complexity of the new fighter but its high-
altitude speed and ruggedness quickly
endeared it to them.

At this time, in the spring of 1942, the War
Production Board began to seek a second
source for Thunderbolts, not just to increase
production but also to ensure that there were
factories situated away from the coast and
apparent vulnerability. Thus a new site was
selected in Evansville, Indiana, in a farmer's
field adjacent to the city' municipal airport. On
19 September 1942, just five months after
ground was first broken for the new factory, the
latter went into full production and the first P-
47 rolled off its assembly line. The first
Indiana-built P-47 was appropriately named
'Hoosier Spirit', and this division consistently
produced P-47s ahead of schedule.

The P-47C and D

At the end of 1942 the P-47C made its début:
this was the first Thunderbolt model that
could truly be considered combat-worthy. The
P-47C was a much improved version of the B
model, the major changes being a quick-
engine-change mount which extended the
fuselage by 13in; reinforced, all-metal-
covered control surfaces; redesigned rudder
and elevator balances (the P-47 still
experienced compressibility problems in
power dives which could prove fatal); and the
addition of shackles to carry a 200 US gallon
external fuel tank on the fuselage underside
(increasing combat range but also raising the
weight to 14,924lb). The early P-47Cs used the
same engine as the B but later versions used
the R-2800-59 with water injection. The C had a
maximum speed of 420mph and a range of 835
miles. A total of 602 were built, and by the end
of 1942 Republic reported over $1 million in
profits for the year, the company thus
declaring the first cash dividend on its
common stock (25 cents a share).

Some P-47Cs eventually saw combat in
Europe, the first arriving in January 1943. One
major problem for the early P-47s in Europe
was their inadequate range. The P-47 was
originally conceived as a high-altitude
interceptor but, in Europe, fighters were
needed for long-range bomber escort. The
P-38 was originally intended for this role but
limited production and the demands of other
theatres of the war delayed its availability,
and the P-47 was pressed into service –
despite the fact that its endurance was limited
to two hours under operational conditions.

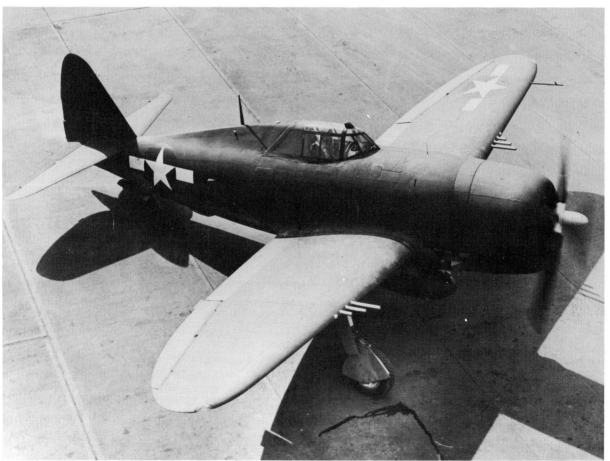

Left: The P-47C, the first Thunderbolt model to see combat in Europe. The early P-47s experienced many teething problems, especially with their engines, and severe limitations were placed on range since the aircraft lacked external fuel tanks. They were first operational with the 56th FG in England. Note the narrow Curtiss-Electric propeller.
Below left: The P-47D was the most numerous of all Thunderbolt models. This early 'Razorback' version clearly shows off the massive, eight-gun fire power of the P-47.
Below: Newly developed, bazooka-like 4.5in High-Velocity Aircraft Rockets (HVAR) were soon fitted on underwing mounts to some P-47Ds in England in the summer of 1944.

The range problem did not become acute until the advent of the long-range B-17 missions in the summer of 1943, when the P-47s could not escort the bombers all the way to their targets and back. Now, clearly, something better was called for.

On 13 October 1941, the further improved P-47D was ordered. This was to become the most famous of all Thunderbolt models as Republic engineers continued to improve the breed. The P-47D proved itself to be incredibly tough, and with its eight machine guns its firepower was deadly to the point of overkill. The introduction of water-injection for emergency power, a new, large-diameter paddle blade propeller and doubled range, plus a bubble canopy giving improved visibility, brought the P-47 to a high level of refinement as a weapon system.

The P-47D was the major production model and over three-quarters of all Thunderbolts were of this version, the first example rolling off Evansville's line in December 1942. Outwardly the early P-47Ds appeared iden-

tical to the C but there were several major internal improvements. More armour plate was added to the cockpit and the exhaust gas system for the turbo-supercharger was redesigned. By the end of 1943 P-47 production had reached its peak of 660 aircraft a month and throughout the following year the daily average would be over twenty – almost one P-47 an hour! However, the demand for P-47s was so great that even two Republic plants could not keep up with it. Thus Curtiss-Wright in Buffalo was called upon to produce the P-47, beginning in early 1943. The Curtiss-built aircraft were D models but they carried the designation P-47G. Their production ended early in 1944 but the 354 produced were assigned to training units in the United States. Two Curtiss P-47Gs were modified into experimental two-seaters: the main fuel tank was reduced in size and a second cockpit added above it, the cabin then being extended forward over the new cockpit.

The most important engineering advance in the D model was the development of large

Above left: This view of a P-47D landing clearly shows the beautiful elliptical wing, the wheel wells and the large flaps. Left: American and British P-47s roll off Republic's line in 1944. Above: Testing a new P-47D at Farmingdale.

external fuel tanks. The early P-47Ds incorporated belly shackles, but after the P-47D-11-RE wing pylons were also added to allow the Thunderbolt to carry two 1,000lb bombs, three 500lb bombs or up to three external fuel tanks. The wing structure was also reinforced, to allow a total external load of up to 2,500lb. The largest ventral external tank that could be carried held 375 US gallons and some units in the field also fabricated 108 US gallon wing tanks which greatly increased the P-47's range. Late-model P-47Ds were also given rails for five rockets on each wing.

When the P-47 first reached the Front, the popular assumption was that the aircraft had to stay at high altitude to survive. Pilots of the Eighth Air Force did not find this to be the case, however, and they completed many missions at low altitude destroying targets of opportunity. To increase the aircraft's low-altitude performance a 13ft-diameter, paddle-bladed Curtiss Electric propeller was added in 1944 and from the P-47D-20 onwards this propeller, combined with water-methanol injection, became standard. Water-injection in the carburettor, automatically engaged when the throttle lever was pushed past the last $1/8$in of its travel, was incorporated to draw more power from the R-2800: put simply, it permitted a leaner mixture of gasoline and air to be used, as the water absorbed much of the heat produced by high combustion. The explosion of fuel in the cylinders was thus

Left: P-47s in various
stages of construction in
Building 17, Republic's
main plant.

slowed down, resulting in a brief, 15 per cent boost in power and increasing the horsepower to 2,535 and the top speed to 433mph. Water-injected engines were classified as R-2800-63 and the wide paddle-bladed propeller allowed the extra power to be used more efficiently; another benefit was the addition of 400ft a minute to the P-47's climb rate.

The typical P-47D had a length of 36ft 1in and a wing span of 40ft 9in. Its top speed was 429mph, with a ceiling of 42,000ft. The total internal fuel capacity was 305 US gallons, later increased to 370, giving a range in excess of 1,000 miles. The P-47D's armament consisted of eight 0.50-calibre machine guns and its

maximum weight was 17,000lb. The D started out with a 2,000hp R-2800-21 radial air-cooled engine, replaced by a 2,300hp R-2800-59 by the time production ended.

During 1943 Republic employees 'paid for' five P-47s, through War Bond Pledges, as did seven US cities. On 1 September that year, with production proceeding at full speed at Farmingdale and Evansville, Ralph Damon stepped down a President and Alfred Marchev took his place. Also in September Republic was awarded its second Army-Navy 'E' flag for excellence in production, its first having been won in 1942. On 7 December, the second anniversary of Pearl Harbor, the 1,000th P-47

Left: Republic Field in
1943. Much new
construction is evident
since the Seversky days
and the runways are now
paved. Note the
camouflaged factories.

Top left: An impressive line-up of P-47Ds at Republic's Farmingdale factory in 1944.
Top right: A P-47 'War Bond' aircraft under construction. The turbo-supercharger area is visible.
Above left: The starboard wing is attached to a razorback P-47D.
Above right: A P-47D's cockpit – by fighter standards unusually roomy and containing a large number of switches and controls.

rolled off for the lines at the Evansville plant to give it an average of fifty machines a month for the first twenty months of its operations; by the spring of 1944 Evansville was accounting for 40 per cent of all Thunderbolt production. Republic's 1943 sales totalled over $283 million.

The early P-47Ds were similar in appearance to the P-47B and C in that the high cockpit and humped-back fuselage blended into the tail via a 'razorback' spine which, although aerodynamically efficient, created a 20-degree blind spot to the rear which could, clearly, reduce a pilot's chances of survival in combat. In order to give all-round vision and eliminate this blind spot, Republic engineers fitted one P-47 with a 'bubble' canopy taken directly from a British Hawker Typhoon; the trial installation was made on the last of the original batch of P-47Ds at Farmingdale, a P-47D-5-RE, in July 1943. Redesignated the XP-47K, this aircraft proved so successful that the

modification was introduced to the production line on all Thunderbolts beginning with the P-47D-25. However, a notable change in the contours of the P-47 resulted. The rear decking was cut down and the radio equipment re-sited, giving the fuselage a much slimmer and more streamlined form. The new configuration created problems of longitudinal stability, but these were corrected by the addition of a long dorsal fillet on later Ds and all following models; subsequent P-47Ds also incorporated two extra oxygen bottles, repositioned cockpit switches, a larger main fuel tank and provision for underwing launchers for ten unguided rockets. The rockets were intended for the ground attack role – in which the P-47 would prove itself particularly effective. Late-series P-47Ds were the second most numerous Thunderbolt variant produced, 6,293 rolling off Republic's lines; in all, 12,602 P-47Ds of all subvariants were built.

Left: The one and only P-47K – a standard razorback P-47D modified with a Typhoon bubble canopy in July 1943; this was the shape all subsequent Thunderbolts were to take. Removing the spine affected the aircraft's stability, but the problem was later solved by the addition of a dorsal fillet; the P-47K lacks this modification.
Below: Neat rows of P47s line Republic Field in 1943. Thunderbolts rolled from the production lines in vast numbers all through the Second World War.

Experimental and late-production Thunderbolts

The Thunderbolt evolved through several further experimental and production versions. In the spring of 1942 a P-47B was taken from the production line and completed with a pressurized cockpit; designated XP-47E, it was part of a research programme seeking a high-altitude escort fighter, the intake for the pressurization unit being located in the port wing root. The XP-47E, which had a hinged canopy similar to that of the XP-47B, proceeded no further than the prototype stage but it did provide some valuable information which would later be put to good use.

Another P-47B was modified into the XP-47F. This aircraft featured a low-drag, laminar-flow wing of a completely new shape and increased span, though, in the event, this offered insufficient advantages over the standard aerofoil to warrant further investigation. A purely experimental design, the XP-47F had no armament. During 1942 and 1943 the aircraft was tested at Wright Field and Langley Field, Virginia, in order to obtain data on the new wing, but the XP-47F proved to be a very unstable aircraft and it crashed on 14 October 1943, killing the pilot.

Its large size and inherent fitness for high performance made the P-47 airframe an ideal test-bed structure for different engines in the quest for greater fighter speeds. The XP-47H, an awkward-looking aircraft, was produced to evaluate the 2,500hp Chrysler XIV-2220-1 sixteen-cylinder, inverted-vee, liquid-cooled engine. Two aircraft were thus modified, from P-47Ds taken from the line in late 1943, and eventually reached a speed of 490mph in

level flight. The XP-47H was delayed for several months while the Chrysler engine was tested and installed, the first flight not taking place until 26 July 1945. No armament was ever fitted in the aircraft, which was never developed further as the Chrysler engine failed to reach production.

Faster still was the XP-47J. This was a greatly modified P-47D – essentially a high-speed, lightweight version of the Thunderbolt – constructed in 1943 as a result of an investigation into how the P-47 design might be simplified. The aircraft was powered by a Pratt & Whitney R-2800-57 'C' engine of 2,800hp which was designed in order to obtain higher power without changes in size or weight. The R-2800-57 'C' in the XP-47J had a fan to force-cool the engine, allowing the use of a redesigned, more streamlined, close-fitting cowling. The supercharger was also given a seperate ventral intake. Many of the changes in the XP-47J were aimed at reducing weight. The armament was reduced from eight guns to six, a smaller, 287 US gallon fuel tank was fitted and all the wing pylons and shackles for external stores were eliminated – modifications which took over 200lb from the weight of the airframe. The aircraft made its first flight on 26 November 1943 and by the spring of 1944, with the help of a more powerful CH-5 supercharger and a propeller of larger diameter, speeds approaching 500mph were being attained. Then, on 5 August 1944, the XP-47J achieved a speed of 504mph in level flight – the highest attained by a propeller-driven aircraft to date, albeit aided by minimum loading. The reason the XP-47J was not placed into production was that this would have required a major change in tooling by Republic which would, in turn, have caused delays in the delivery of standard P-47s – which was unacceptable to the USAAF; moreover, the XP-47J was superseded by a superior Republic high-speed fighter, the XP-72.

In the autumn of 1943 it was apparent that the range of escort fighters in the Pacific needed to be increased, and Republic, accordingly, enlarged the P-47's internal fuel tanks. The last production P-47D-20-RE served as the trials aircraft for a redesigned fuel tank holding an additional 65 US gallons; incorporating other minor refinements, this machine was redesignated XP-47L. In early 1944 the improvements worked into both the XP-47K and the XP-47L were adopted as

standard, although no new model type designation was given. These Thunderbolts were slightly slower than earlier P-47Ds but the extra fuel gave them over 200 more miles in range (now over 1,000 miles) and an hour more in endurance.

The appearance of the jet-propelled V1 flying bomb and the Messerschmitt Me 262 fighter over Europe called for the development of a high-speed 'sprint' version of the P-47D, and in the spring of 1944 three such aircraft were fitted out with the 2,800hp R-2800-57 engine used in the XP-47J, a more powerful CH-5 turbo-supercharger and a number of automatic engine controls and were designated YP-47M. A total of 130 P-47Ms were built and these were intended for interception duties only as no external ordnance could be carried and the overall weight was reduced. Their range was limited to 530 miles but speeds of 470mph – 50mph in excess of that of the P-47D and the highest of any production Thunderbolt – could be reached. The P-47M was also equipped with air brakes under its wings for rapid deceleration after the aircraft had dived on its target. Virtually all the P-47Ms built eventually went to the 56th Fighter Group based in Britain, although because of persistent problems with ignition leads, turbo-regulators and engines they did not begin to see full-scale operations until April 1945. In the last days of the European war the P-47M did some notable work, and on several occasions it caught and shot down Me 262s.

On 20 September 1944, with suitable ceremonies, the 10,000th P-47 was rolled off Republic's assembly lines; Jacqueline Cochran, then Chief of the WASP Ferry Pilot Service, christened it 'Ten Grand'. By the end of 1944 Republic had expanded from 5,900 employees in 1941 (over 30 per cent of them women) to 24,450 and the two plants together produced 5,200 aircraft in that one year. Republic had also steadily cut the number of man-hours required to produce a single P-47, from an average of 22,925 for the first 773 aircraft to 6,290 for 'Ten Grand'; over the same time, the unit cost had been reduced from an average of $68,750 to $45,600. At the end of 1944 Republic's two factories were producing 28 P-47s per day and the value of unfulfilled orders stood at $475 million. By July 1945 'Fifteen Grand' had rolled off the assembly lines, marking the production of 5,000 P-47s in the ten months since 'Ten Grand' had been completed.

Right: The final version of the P-47D. The bubble canopy greatly improved the pilot's vision out of the cockpit and thus increased his chances of survival in combat. This brand new Thunderbolt was photographed over peaceful Long Island countryside.

Right: The XP-47F, an experimental Thunderbolt with a laminar-flow wing. Only one was built, it was not very successful and it eventually crashed, killing the pilot.

Right: Two experimental two-seat P-47Gs were built by Curtiss-Wright in Buffalo. The ample fuselage of the P-47 required little modification to fit in the second cockpit. The G model was equipped with dual controls and intended as a primary trainer but the programme did not progress beyond the testing stage.

Above left: Wartime demands called for better performance in the P-47 and the XP-47J was created in response. This model was fitted with a more powerful fan-cooled engine and high-thrust supercharger but despite setting a new speed record of 505mph on 5 August 1944 the P-47J never went into production – mainly because of an anticipated delay in re-tooling and the good prospects of the forthcoming XP-72.
Centre left: Probably the ugliest P-47 built was the XP-47H. In the quest for more power, two P-47Ds were adapted to accept water-cooled Chrysler V16 engines of 2,500hp. However, there was virtually no improvement in performance and the war ended before all the 'bugs' were worked out.
Bottom left: The P-47M was the high-powered version of the P-47D; here the No. 2 aircraft is seen during trials at Farmingdale. All 130 P-47Ms went to the 56th FG in England.
Above: The P-47N, the last production model of the Thunderbolt, was a long-range variant designed for use in the Pacific and almost 2,000 were built before the war ended. This particular N is an early machine, lacking the dorsal fillet.

During 1944 there was a continuing need to increase the range of escort fighters in the Pacific, and this led to the final mass-produced Thunderbolt variant, the P-47N, which had the longest range of any model but, at 21,200lb, was also the heaviest. The P-47N was given a distinctive, 42ft 6in span, square-tipped wing containing two additional 96 US gallon fuel tanks in the inner panels and first tested on the XP-47K. Republic eventually built 1,817 P-47Ns, principally intended as escorts for B-29 Superfortresses in the Pacific: with a 300 US gallon external ventral tank, the N had a combat range of 2,300 miles, whilst with full internal fuel and up to four underwing external tanks it could remain aloft for up to nine hours. It could carry three 500lb bombs and ten unguided rockets, and had a top speed of 467mph.

The XP-47N first flew in July 1944 and eventually all P-47 production was switched to this model. It was fitted with the R-2800-77 engine in conjunction with the improved CH-5 turbo-supercharger, and further improvements included an oxygen capacity increased by 80 per cent, automatic operation of the intercooler doors, automatic operation of the water injection, C-1 automatic engine controls and an undercarriage of wider track. The P-47N proved to be a highly reliable airframe and engine combination as well as being a simpler and less demanding Thunderbolt to fly compared with previous models. The P-47 production line ceased to operate in November 1945 and the last few Thunderbolts were delivered the next month. The overall production of the P-47 reached a grand total of

15,683, exceeding that of any other fighter acquired by the US Air Corps/Forces.

The XP-69

Concurrent with the development of the P-47, Republic was also working on two other experimental fighters. A few weeks after the XP-47B first flew, Republic initiated a new fighter project designated AP-18. Essentially a more advanced version of the earlier AP-12 Rocket proposal, this was intended as a high-speed, high-altitude local defence interceptor to protect American bases and cities against enemy bombers. Thus it was to be heavily armed, and equipped with a pressurized cockpit. In late 1941 the Air Corps ordered two AP-18 prototypes, now redesignated XP-69, and by June 1942 Republic had completed a three-quarter scale mock-up.

The XP-69 was to be powered by a 42-cylinder, six-row, air-cooled Wright 2160 radial engine of 2,500hp, buried in the aircraft's mid-fuselage, aft of the pilot, and cooled by air ducted through a large ventral intake. Power was to be transmitted to a pair of 13ft 8in-diameter contra-rotating propellers via a long extension shaft passing beneath the cockpit, the latter located well forward of the wing; the aircraft was also to be equipped with a turbo-supercharger, in order to attain high altitudes. The Kartveli influence was clearly evident in the streamlined empennage, and this was continued through to the XF-12 Rainbow and the P-84 Thunderjet. The armament of the XP-69 was to be two big 37mm cannon in the nose and four 0.50-calibre machine guns in the wings.

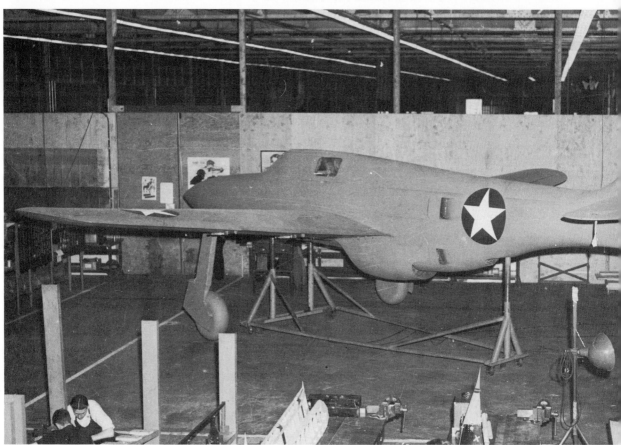

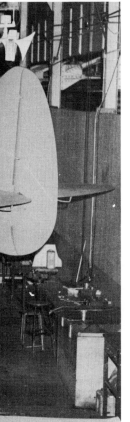

Above left: For publicity purposes, one P-47N was assembled as a 'cutaway' aircraft for display in Republic's factory. Note the complex system of 'plumbing' to the supercharger.
Above: Three sleek new P-47Ns fly in formation. All P-47Ns were distinguished by their squared-off wing tips and most had the long dorsal fillet.
Left: In a secure, walled-off area of Republic's factory the three-quarter scale mock-up of the monster XP-69 takes shape. This design was to feature a buried, water-cooled, 42-cylinder Wright engine and would weigh about ten tons.

The XP-69 would have been a real monster: with a wing span of 51ft 8in and an overall length of 51ft 6in it would have been bigger than the P-38. Its maximum weight would have been 26,164lb but with only 2,500hp available its intended speed of 450mph seems optimistic. Service ceiling was to have been 48,900ft and fuel capacity up to 700 US gallons. In May 1943 the USAAF cancelled the XP-69 contract: Republic was already working on a more advanced P-47 design, the XP-72, which looked much more promising, involved less retooling and would have been far cheaper than the XP-69.

The XP-72

The search for greater aircraft speeds culminated in the 3,500hp Pratt & Whitney R-4360 Wasp Major – the most powerful piston engine to reach production status during the Second World War. This generated 1,000 more horsepower than was available to standard P-47s and so when Republic engineers were considering a way of improving the Thunderbolt they turned to this new unit. Design studies began in July 1941, two months after the XP-47B first took to the air; by June 18 1943 the USAAF felt that the prospects of the new design were sufficiently promising, a development contract was signed and two prototype XP-72s were ordered.

The first XP-72, flown on 2 February 1944, appeared quite similar to the P-47D, differing principally in the narrower nose created when the supercharger intake was moved back beneath the wing. The 28-cylinder R-4360-13 was contained in a tight-fitting, streamlined cowling and was force-cooled by a fan located behind the spinner. As in the P-47D, the supercharger was located in the fuselage rear, but the fuselage was deeper on account of the intake fairing. Several features which proved worthwhile on the P-47D were also incorporated in the XP-72, including the 'bubble' canopy and recovery flaps for slowing the aircraft as it approached the speed of sound in a dive.

The first XP-72 utilized a conventional four-bladed propeller but the second was built with contra-rotating Aero Products 13ft 6in propellers. During their flight test programme, the two XP-72s showed outstanding performance characteristics, reaching speeds of up to 490mph, and a contract for 100 production aircraft was issued. However, in short order the USAAF revised its fighter requirements in favour of a long-range bomber escort such as the P-47N and the contract was cancelled.

The XP-72 had a wing span of 40ft 11in and a length of 36ft 7in and weighed 11,500lb; its service ceiling was 42,000ft. The prototypes were armed with six 0.50-calibre machine guns instead of eight, in order to keep the weight down, while production P-72s were to have carried four 37mm cannon as well as two 1,000lb bombs under the wings. Fuel capacity was 370 US gallons, which gave a range of 1,200

miles. The big Pratt & Whitney's fuel comsumption limited the XP-72's range and the advent of jets rendered its 490mph speed unspectacular.

The P-47 in combat

The first P-47s arrived in England a few days before Christmas 1942, 88 machines being issued to the Eighth Air Force. They were originally assigned to the 4th, 56th and 78th Fighter Groups – the three 'Eagle Squadrons', composed of Amercians who had previously flown with the RAF. As most of these pilots were converting from aircraft such as Spitfires, they disliked the P-47 at first, finding it big, complicated, sluggish and unmanoeuvrable; furthermore, they experienced engine problems because of the cool, moist British air. However, the 56th Fighter Group liked their P-47s as they had trained on them in America and were thus more familiar with their eccentricities.

The first operational P-47 fighter sweep, by the 4th Fighter Group, took place on 10 March 1943 and the unit's first brush with the *Luftwaffe* occurred on 15 April. On that day the 4th Group, led by Maj. Donald Blakeslee, downed three Fw 190s for the first P-47 victories. However, over the next few weeks several P-47s were lost in combat as a result of engine failure: apparently the cylinder heads were being blown when full power was applied. A system of automatic safeguards was eventually devised as an aid against high manifold boost. On 4 May P-47s went on their first escort mission with B-17s in a raid on Antwerp. Soon the pilots' confidence in the aircraft grew and they began to make their presence felt while escorting mass bomber formations over Europe. One thing that helped to convince pilots that the Thunderbolt was a good aircraft was its ability to take punishment and get back home. Damaged P-47s that returned were living testimony to the aircraft's solid contruction.

On 29 June 1943 Capt. Charles London shot down two Messerschmitt Bf 109s to bring his total to five and thus become the first P-47 ace. German fighters proved to be unable to escape from a P-47 in a dive as they had previously from Spitfires. Another of the Thunderbolt's advantages was its massive firepower: with a two-second burst from its eight machine guns it could bring down an enemy aircraft. From August 1943 on, the 56th Fighter Group, led by Col. Hubert Zemke,

were a force to be reckoned with. Once its members had learned to use the speed and firepower of the P-47 to their advantage, the 56th's record of air combat was never surpassed by any US Group in Europe. By the end of July 1943, P-47s had destroyed 33 German aircraft.

The initial P-47 squadrons were followed by the 80th and 348th Groups. In June 1943 the 348th went to Australia and with the Fifth Air Force conducted a highly successful campaign against Japanese forces. These P-47s served as escorts to bombers destroying Japanese airfields in New Guinea. The Thunderbolts could not hope to outmanoeuvre Japanese fighters in a turning combat so they developed the very successful tactic of diving on the enemy from altitude, attacking and zooming away. The Japanese aircraft's vulnerability to incendiary ammunition allowed the P-47 to open fire at twice the range compared with German fighters. In September P-47s covered MacArthur's landing at Lae in New Guinea.

On 11 October 1943 the 348th Group Commander, Lt. Col. Neel Kearby, destroyed six Japanese aircraft single-handedly in one action and was consequently awarded the Congressional Medal of Honor – the first to an Air Forces fighter pilot. By the end of 1943 some 300 P-47s were in Australia and New Guinea as four Fifth Air Force squadrons converted from the P-39 and P-40, supporting the re-conquest of New Guinea and the

Left: Seeking even greater speed, Republic produced the XP-72 – the ultimate development of the Thunderbolt. Designed around the 3,000hp Pratt & Whitney R-4360, the aircraft achieved speeds of around 490mph. The tight-fitting cowling required a fan to force-cool the engine and it was necessary to take off and land in a three-point attitude to avoid damaging the propeller. Six guns were used instead of eight to save weight, and the supercharger intake was also located much further aft than hitherto.

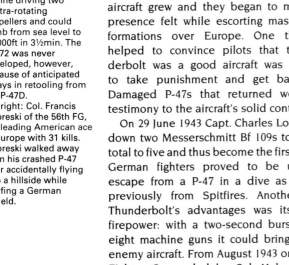

Left: The second XP-72 incorporated the same engine driving two contra-rotating propellers and could climb from sea level to 15,000ft in 3½min. The XP-72 was never developed, however, because of anticipated delays in retooling from the P-47D.
Far right: Col. Francis Gabreski of the 56th FG, the leading American ace in Europe with 31 kills. Gabreski walked away from his crashed P-47 after accidentally flying into a hillside while strafing a German airfield.

Philippines and attacking ground targets prior to the invasions of Leyte and Luzon. Range was critical over the vast expanses of jungle and ocean, and the P-47 was a great improvement over earlier aircraft.

Meanwhile by the end of 1943 the Eighth Air Force in England had some ten P-47 groups, rising to twenty by May 1944; totaling 1,800 aircraft, the P-47 was now the prevalent type of American combat aircraft based in that country. The introduction of locally made 108 US gallon drop tanks in September 1943 was a major advance, enabling P-47s to fly all the way to Emden and giving B-17s and B-24s continuous fighter cover for 325 miles into enemy territory. A 150 US gallon external tank was introduced in February 1944, just in time for 'Big Week' (20–25 February). During this time the P-47s provided escort for the massive bomber raids against manufacturing centres all across Germany, while in March that year they escorted the first American daylight mission against Berlin.

Ground-attack Thunderbolts

By January 1944 enough P-47s and pilots were available that they could begin to be used for other types of mission, such as dive-bombing and level bombing. The Thunderbolt's success in attacking ground targets led in March 1944 to the establishment of a special flight of P-47s expressly for the purpose of attacking airfields, trains and other tactical targets, the intention being to destroy the transport system in France prior to the Allied invasion. It was found that, in order to be successful, surprise and low-altitude flying were essential. In April 1944 other Ninth Air Force P-47 Groups underwent similar intensive training and within a month these Groups were daily bombing bridges, tunnels, trains and railway yards. The Thunderbolt, with its massive structure, reliable engine and eight guns, was ideally suited to the ground attack role; furthermore, the introduction of water-injection and a paddle-bladed propeller gave it good performance at low altitude. During the Allied landings in June 1944 P-47s helped to keep away the *Luftwaffe* and form a protective screen around the beach-heads. They also destroyed bridges and made rail cuts, slowing the reinforcement of German troops, and bombed and strafed German lines, tanks and gun emplacements, helping in the US breakout. By the end of June the first P-47 airfield was established on the

Left: Col. Robert Johnson, also of the 56th, was the second leading American ace in Europe with 28 kills. Johnson greatly appreciated the ruggedness of his P-47.
Right: The ace and his steed: Robert Johnson and his P-47D in England. The fact that the two leading American aces in Europe flew the P-47 is a tribute to the aircraft's speed, fire power and ruggedness.

Left: 'Fightin Gator', one of the many P-47s purchased with the proceeds of War Bond sales to Republic employees. The aircraft was assigned to the 404th FG and flew 200 missions over Europe. Pilot R. Schaefer, pictured here, flew the aircraft's last mission from Belgium.
Right: One photograph says it all: a low-flying P-47 streaks over American troops while supporting ground operations in Europe in 1945.

Left: 'Ten Grand', the 10,000th P-47 built. It served with Col. Gladwyn Pinkston and the Twelfth Air Force in Italy.

Left: The P-47 was renowned for its ability to take major damage and still get the pilot back home. A direct anti-aircraft hit failed to down this P-47 and it made a successful belly landing at its home airfield.

continent. Throughout 1944, as the ground troops advanced, P-47s of the Ninth Air Force acted as their aerial extension.

The P-47's fighter-bomber duties proved beyond doubt its ability to take many hits and keep flying: fighters such as the Spitfire, Typhoon and Mustang with their liquid-cooled engines were by comparison vulnerable to enemy fire, but the P-47's R-2800 could sustain major damage and keep running. A P-47 pilot's chances of survival were undoubtedly better than in any other type of fighter and the following description by ace Robert Johnson clearly demonstrates the aircraft's ruggedness:*

They insist on taking me to the hospital at once. Not yet; I want to look over the P-47. And this airplane is not a pretty sight. My awe and respect for the fighter increase as I walk around the battered machine.

Left: On 23 June 1944 Thunderbolts of the 318th FG were successfully catapulted from the deck of the USS *Manila Bay* and landed directly on Saipan. The aircraft subsequently flew many combat missions during the conquest of the Mariana Islands.

There are twenty-one gaping holes and jagged tears in the metal from exploding 20mm cannon shells. I'm still standing in one place when my count of the bullet holes reaches past a hundred; there's no use even trying to add them all. The Thunderbolt is literally a sieve, holes through the wings, nose, fuselage and tail. Every square foot, it seems, is covered with holes. There are five holes in the propeller. Three 20mm cannon shells burst against the armor plate, a scant inch away from my head. Five cannon shell holes in the right wing, four in the left wing. Two cannon shells blasted away the lower half of my rudder. One shell exploded in the cockpit, next to my left hand; this is the blast that ripped away the flap handle. More holes appear along the fuselage and in the tail. Behind the cockpit the metal is twisted and curled; this had jammed the canopy, trapping me inside.

The airplane had done her best. Needless to say, she would never fly again.

In July 1944 the USAAF installed 4.5in rockets on P-47s. Essentially a development of an infantry weapon, this installation featured a cluster of three bazooka-like launching tubes slung beneath each wing. The weapon at first proved difficult to aim and had a detrimental effect upon performance, but the tubes were aligned with the wing guns and eventually the rockets were used to good effect against German tanks and trucks. P-47s were later fitted with ten 5in High Velocity Aircraft Rockets (HVAR) requiring neither rails nor guides.

In January 1944 the Twelfth Air Force in Italy began operations with six P-47 Groups, the first being the 325th at Foggia. The Twelfth concentrated on air–ground operations in a very successful interdiction campaign behind enemy lines. Here, the P-47 was also used by the 332nd Group, the only group of black fighter pilots in the Army Air Forces.

By May 1944 only four P-47 Fighter Groups – the 56th, 78th, 353rd and 356th – were left with the Eighth Air Force in Britain; most of the other Groups had converted to the P-51 Mustang, which had a greater range and could escort bombers all the way to their targets. The remaining P-47 Groups were available for the needs of Allied commands, such as destroying anti-aircraft gun positions in the Netherlands during the airborne landings in September 1944. By January 1945 only the 56th was still flying the P-47, having been supplied with 130 fast but problematic P-47Ms. Nevertheless the 56th was the highest-scoring Group in the Eighth Air Force, with 674 enemy aircraft destroyed; it also had the two leading American aces in Europe, Francis Gabreski

with 31 kills and Robert Johnson with 28, together with five other pilots with over fifteen victories apiece.

Meanwhile the Twelfth Air Force's P-47s provided close air support during the Allied invasion of Southern France in the summer of 1944. They then returned to the difficult Italian battle front. The 1st Fighter Squadron of the Brazilian Air Force also flew P-47s in Italy during the final six months of the war, while Thunderbolts of the Ninth Air Force flew operations up to 8 May 1945, mostly against German airfields. P-47s served on other fronts during the war. A total of 203 were sent to the Soviet Union in 1944 and they were apparently used against the Germans, though with unknown results; and in 1944 eight P-47 squadrons were operating in Burma, supporting ground troops and flying partial cover along 'The Hump', and another two were in India.

Pacific Thunderbolts

After the defeat of Germany in May 1945, only the 58th and 318th Groups were still flying the P-47 in the Pacific. At times they flew sorties of over 800 miles in order to sweep targets for Japanese fighters before the bombers arrived. In order to ensure prompt support for ground troops during the invasion of the Marianas, 318th FG P-47s were loaded on to two escort carriers in Hawaii in June 1944. All 71 aircraft were successfully catapulted from the carrier decks and they landed on Saipan with the enemy still on the island. This Group later supported ground troops during the invasions of Tinian and Guam.

In April 1945 the 318th converted to the longer-range P-47N and flew, in stages, 4,100 miles to Ie Shima, only 325 miles from the Japanese homeland. During June two other P-47N Groups, the 413th and 507th, joined the 318th in order to provide escort for B-29 Superfortresses striking Japan. However, the capabilities of the P-47 in the ground-attack role meant that it was rarely assigned to escort duties: more often it was given the task of destroying anything Japanese that could move on land or sea, such as railway traffic, parked aircraft and shipping. Only once did all three Groups escort a massive daylight B-29 raid, that on 8 August 1945 to Yawata. The leading P-47 ace in the Pacific was Neel Kearby with 22 victories.

---

*Johnson, Robert. *Thunderbolt*. Rinehart & Co. (New York, 1958)

When hostilities ceased in Europe over 3,000 P-47s were stationed there, mostly D models; at the time of Japan's surrender, 1,400 P-47s were scattered through the Pacific theatre.

After the US Army Air Forces, the RAF was the largest operator of P-47s during the Second World War. Over 800 were transferred to the British under Lend-Lease, most being sent to South-East Asia. The P-47 was originally offered to the RAF as a high-altitude interceptor, for which it had no need, but the service did see the aircraft's usefulness as a tactical fighter. The first 240 supplied were P-47D-20s ('razorback'), designated Thunderbolt I by the British. These were mostly shipped direct from the United States to India. The first RAF squadron to begin P-47 operations was No. 146, in May 1944 on the Burma Front, and by the end of that year Thunderbolt IIs, with a 'bubble' canopy, had arrived, in sufficient numbers to equip nine squadrons. Nearly all were used for ground support of the British Fourteenth Army, dive-bombing and strafing enemy airfields and escorting cargo-carrying C-47s. Combat with Japanese aircraft was rare. Most of the RAF P-47 pilots had previously flown Hurricanes and Spitfires. They found the P-47 less manoeuvrable and they also disliked its poor forward visibility while taxiing and its long take-off runs in the Pacific heat, but they enjoyed its stability,

Above: A British Thunderbolt Mk I (P-47D) of No 134 Squadron in India, late 1944.

Below: A brand new Thunderbolt Mk II for the RAF sits at the Republic plant in 1944.

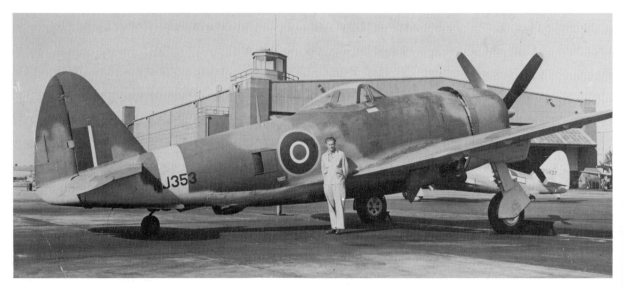

Above: P-47Ns were rarely used for bomber-escort in the Pacific theatre: their heavy firepower and load-carrying ability made them much more suitable for interdiction missions. This N carries two 500lb bombs and ten 'Tiny Tim' rockets.

Below: New P-47Ds destined for service in Britain and Brazil.

firepower, ruggedness, range, roomy cockpit and reliable air-cooled engine. The last RAF Thunderbolts to see action were used against Indonesian rebles in Java in November 1945.

Peace: surpluses and cancellations
Between March 1943 and August 1945 P-47s flew 546,000 combat sorties, dropped 132,000 tons of bombs and fired 60,000 rockets. In Europe they destroyed 86,000 railway wagons, 9,000 locomotives, 68,000 trucks and 6,000 armoured vehicles and tanks. Thunderbolts also established a 4.6:1 kill ratio over German aircraft, destroying 7,000 of the latter (air and ground) in the process. Two-thirds of all P-47s built were sent to combat theatres and

operational losses amounted to 3,499 aircraft.
On 14 August 1945 both Republic plants received the news that the war was over. The management then ordered an immediate ten-day shutdown of both plants. After the closure about half of all Republic's employees were laid off (and virtually all the women) because of a drastic cutback in P-47 orders: in all, the war's end led to the cancellation of 5,943 P-47Ns. On 9 November 1945 the last P-47 built, an N model, rolled off Republic's assembly lines; this aircraft now resides at the Cradle of Aviation Museum, just a short distance from the Farmingdale factory. In total, some 15,683 Thunderbolts were built, 6,242 of these at Evansville, and during the war the

manufacturers received seven 'E' awards for excellence in production.

At the end of the Second World War there existed a huge surplus of P-47s, far beyond the future needs of the US Army Air Forces. The best way of disposing of these aircraft was to sell them cheaply to nations with no aviation industry of their own, and large numbers were sold at bargain rates to, among others, Latin American nations. Among those countries to receive Thunderbolts (mostly late P-47Ds) after 1945 were Bolivia, Brazil, Chile, China, Colombia, Dominica, Ecuador, France, Guatamala, Honduras, Iran, Mexico, Nicaragua, Peru, Portugal, Turkey, Venezuela and Yugoslavia. Some of these P-47s, especially those operated by Central and South American air forces, remained in active service until the mid-1960s.

When the Farmingdale plant re-opened, a

Left: One of over 200 P-47Ds destined for the Soviet Union, 1944. It is unknown what measure of success these aircraft enjoyed on the Eastern Front.

new contract was announced: American airlines had asked Republic to convert fifty C-54 military transports for use as civilian airliners. These Douglas Skymasters had proved dependable in millions of miles of flight under rigorous wartime conditions; now they were to be transformed into luxurious DC-4s for commercial schedules. This contract, which extended well into 1946, enabled Republic to retain 1,500 more employees than had been thought possible with the automatic cancellation of all P-47s other than those nearing completion. The first C-54s began to arrive for conversion in mid-September but the Evansville facility, no longer needed, was returned to the Government's Defense Plant Corporation.

The XF-12 Rainbow

Below: Republic XF-12 No. 1 taking shape in Farmingdale's Building 17 late in 1945. Republic had great hopes for the high-flying reconnaissance aircraft.

Towards the end of 1943, officials at Republic realized that they had to branch out and produce something other than P-47s; Grumman and Boeing, for example, were simultaneously producing several types of aircraft and Republic clearly needed a larger share of the world aviation market. At the same time, in October 1943, the Air Technical Service Command at Wright Field put out a request for a new high-altitude, long-range, high-speed photo-reconnaissance aircraft primarily for use in the Pacific; the USAAF had found that their operations in all theatres were being hindered by the lack of such an aircraft, with intelligence photographs of possible targets and of the results of strikes against targets being the responsibility of several different types of bombers and fighters not designed for the purpose. Alexander Kartveli concluded that the requirements listed could be met by a sleek four-engined aircraft driven by available piston powerplants and he believed that this contract would not only give Republic a chance to build its first multi-engined aircraft but would also open up the possibility of getting into commercial aviation at the same time. The Hughes XF-11 was also a multi-engined response to the Air Forces' request.

Kartveli thus designed the XF-12 Rainbow, possibly the most beautifully streamlined multi-engined aircraft ever built. Designed as a flying photo-laboratory for the Air Forces, the Rainbow was built to match the speeds of fighter aircraft. In March 1944 the USAAF awarded Republic a $6.5 million contract for two XF-12s. A mid-wing design was selected as this offered the minimum of drag. The engine nacelles – which were made as narrow as possible by using engine-driven cooling fans which rammed air into the engines, thus eliminating the need for wide openings – extended as far aft of the wing as forward in order to house a pressure-booster device which compressed exhaust gases, directed them to the rear and thereby added 200hp to each powerplant. The XF-12 also featured a highly streamlined, 'bullet-nosed' fuselage affording excellent visibility. However, the transparent nose was in actuality an unpressurized fairing (the cockpit was equipped with an internal windscreen), the conical halves of which could slide into the fuselage for better visibility during take-off and landing.

The new aircraft had a wing span of 129ft, a fuselage length of 94ft and a fin towering over 28ft above the ground. It was powered by four 28-cylinder Pratt & Whitney R-4360-37 Wasp Major engines, each developing 3,250hp and incorporating single-speed blowers. An exhaust-driven GE turbo-supercharger was located in the rear of each nacelle, these gathering thrust of up to one-third of the

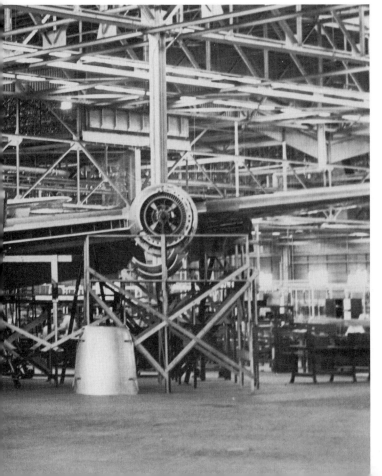

original horsepower. The charge air from each turbo-supercharger was carried forward through an intercooler in the wing leading edge and through the engine blower to the carburettor, the exhaust gases then being ejected at the rear of each nacelle to produce a 'jet effect'. Each engine drove a 16ft-diameter four-bladed Curtiss propeller. The aircraft's fuel capacity of 5,000 US gallons was carried in removable cells in the wings, whilst the engine oil was housed in six tanks located in the nacelles and wing leading edge. By June 1944 the USAAF inspected the first full-scale mock-up of the aircraft, which had been produced in a remarkably short period of time.

The Rainbow was designed to fly at 40,000ft and up to 450mph. For its photo-mission it had three camera stations to permit vertical and split-vertical, trimetrogon pictures and a vertical viewfinder. It also carried complete radio and radar equipment, flash bombs for night photography and dark-room equipment to permit the loading, storing and developing of film in flight – and it was armour-plated. Later, on one occasion, the XF-12 flew non-stop from Edwards AFB, California, to Mitchell Field, Long Island, at 40,000ft, continuously taking photographs so as to get one 200ft-long strip of the United States from coast to coast.

The XF-12 was of all-metal, stressed-skin construction, flush-riveted throughout and utilizing the latest high-strength aluminium alloys. The fuselage was semi-monocoque with transverse frames and longitudinal stringers, built in prefabricated sections and bolted together, and was pressurized from the pilot's compartment through to the aft cabin. The wing was of full-cantilever, two-spar construction with removable outer panels attached just beyond the outboard engine nacelles. The flaps extended over approximately 85 per cent of the span and were of the double-slotted type to obtain the highest possible lift coefficient. Lateral control was obtained by the use of rectractable plug-type spoilers deployed in conjunction with small conventional ailerons which built up forces sufficient to give 'feel' to the controls. Even though the aircraft was of mid-wing contruction there were no through-spars to disrupt the interior: wing loads were transferred to the fuselage through the centre-section frames.

Right: The unpressurized, pencil-point nose of the XF-12 Rainbow clearly reveals the inner windscreen with pressurized cockpit behind it.
Below: A study in streamlining, Republic's XF-12 was powered by four massive 3,500hp R-4360 engines.
Below right: The Rainbow's fuselage could hold a wide variety of photographic equipment, including complete dark room facilities to permit the development and printing of film in flight.

The tail was of full-cantilever design, with a single fin and rudder. In addition to balancing tabs, the reduction of control forces was obtained by means of spring-loaded control tabs. All the control surfaces were of the sealed-gap type to provide a smoother rate of change for the control forces and to reduce all possible drag. The tricycle undercarriage consisted of a double-wheel nose gear, retracting rearwards flush into the fuselage. Each of the two main wheels were nearly 6ft in diameter and retracted laterally into the inboard portion of the wing, not the nacelles. The landing gear doors were similar in configuration to those of the P-47, though much larger. The gear was retracted hydraulically and designed to extend under gravity as a safety feature.

A luxury airliner

With the XF-12 nearing completion as the war ended, Republic's management wisely began to promote the aircraft's potential as a luxurious commercial transport, and an evaluation of its specifications indicated that it could easily become the world's fastest airliner. The company arranged a meeting of airline executives and presented the characteristics of the XF-12, which by now was christened the RC-2 (Republic Commercial 2) Rainbow: it could carry 40 passengers and a crew of seven from New York to London in nine hours, with 1,600lb of baggage and 1,700lb of cargo, in air-conditioned, pressurized comfort whatever the weather; and, touted as the most modern intercontinental airliner yet, it had a range of 4,000 miles, which

Above: The Republic Rainbow takes off on its maiden flight, 4 February 1946. It is still the fastest multi-engine, propeller-driven aircraft ever built. Above right: Each engine nacelle on the XF-12 was the size of a P-47, while the landing gear doors clearly resembled those of that aircraft.

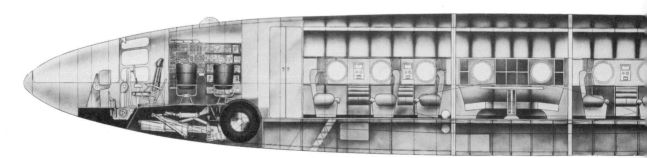

Below: When Air Force contracts appeared to be in jeopardy, Republic touted the Rainbow to America's airlines but only Pan American and American placed orders, for a total of 26 aircraft. Up to 40 passengers would have travelled in pressurized luxury, flying from New York to Los Angeles in a swift eight hours.

would enable it to circle the globe in 45 hours. The Rainbow was judged by airline leaders to exhibit the ideal qualities they were looking for in their drive to press foward after the restrictions of the war years, and the announcement that Republic would enter into contracts with airlines to build the Rainbow was front-page news. The aircraft was scheduled to fly early in 1946.

In January 1946 workmen cut additional space through the top of the big door of Hangar 3 at Farmingdale to give clearance for the towering tail of the Rainbow so that it could be moved from its birthplace. On 4 February the aircraft was hauled out to the flight-line and, as hundreds of Republic employees watched, Chief Test Pilot Lowery Brabham took the pilot's seat. The four

powerful engines lifted the big aeroplane into the air after she had rolled along only one-third of the 5,000ft runway. Once in the air her unusual beauty and aerodynamic symmetry

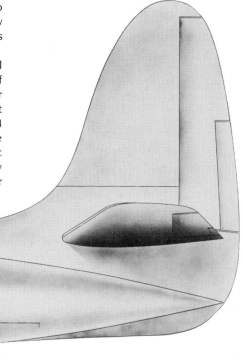

Left: In 1947 Pan American and American Airlines cancelled their Rainbow orders owing to its high purchase and operating costs and the luxury Rainbow liner was to remain only an artist's dream.
Right: Although clean and high-flying, the beautiful Rainbow was eclipsed by the advent of jet aircraft for military purposes and the fact that contemporary civilian airliners cost less and could carry more. The aircraft's most famous flight was a non-stop coast-to-coast sortie continuously taking photographs along the way.

were self-evident. For seventeen minutes the XF-12 was put through her paces. News of the Rainbow's first flight was flashed to airline executives: she was the fastest multi-engined, propeller-driven aircraft ever built.

By the spring of 1946, inspired by Republic's public relations drive, first American Airlines ordered twenty Rainbows, then Pan American ordered six with an option for twelve. The cost for each was to be $1.25 million and deliveries were to begin in 1947. Passenger comfort was the dominant theme in the arrangement of the fuselage, the accommodation providing two double rows of seats, with decor in restful pastel colours. A rear door was provided for the passengers and a front entrance through the floor for the crew, baggage and cargo. Two buffet cabinets and a coat room were to be located near the passenger entrance door, while spacious and luxurious bathrooms, a galley and a bar were to be installed at the rear of the cabin. The pressurized air for the cabin was taken from all four intercoolers, the air passing through a mixing valve regulated by a thermostat to maintain a constant temperature in the cabin. This pressurization

allowed the Rainbow to fly over weather not through it, in contrast to other postwar airliners.

In May 1946 the Rainbow set a new cross-country speed record for four-engined aircraft while on a flight from Wright Field, Ohio, to New York. On the return flight of 576 miles, the Rainbow registered 426mph; the previous best time for a multi-engined aeroplane was 375mph by a Lockheed Constellation. In 1947 an emergency occurred which provided an informative, but unwelcome, illustration of the structural integrity of the Rainbow. In a test of its ability to carry heavy loads, the aircraft was being put through a series of short, simulated emergency landings. Approaching the runway at too steep an angle, the heavily loaded machine broke off its right main landing gear strut. The pilot nevertheless made a skilful landing and the Rainbow sustained minimal damage and was quickly repaired. By August 1947 the second Rainbow had made its maiden flight with a highly successful one-hour sortie over Long Island. Republic was rewarded when, in October 1946, the USAAF ordered twenty F-12s for photo-reconnaissance duties from northern bases in Canada and Alaska.

However, efforts to work out a satisfactory basis for the manufacture of the civil version of

the Rainbow for American Airlines and Pan American ran into difficulty. In making its bid with the Rainbow for the highly competitive commercial transport manufacturing field, Republic had very closely calculated its costs and had worked out contracts with both companies which depended on their placing orders for a sufficient quantity to permit economical tooling and production; the final determination of costs also took into account the extent to which the Air Forces ordered the aircraft in its military photo-reconnaissance version, as this covered a substantial portion of the Rainbow's development cost. None of these factors could be clearly foreseen at the end of 1946, and uncertainty as to the future of the Rainbow was also clouded by politics arising from the debate within the Truman Adminis-tration about the size of the Air Forces' budget.

Throughout 1947 extended negotiations were under way involving the Air Force,* Republic and representatives of American Airlines and Pan American, looking toward both military and commercial production. All four parties wanted to 'dovetail' these contracts so as to spread the aircraft's

*The National Security Act of 18 September 1947 saw the reorganization of the US Army Air Forces into the US Air Force (USAF).

Left: In 1947 a peculiar mishap occurred when an Air Force crew snapped off the starboard main gear of one of the two Rainbows when approaching the runway at too steep an angle. An emergency landing was later made, with comparatively minor damage.

development costs and to make it possible to produce the transport model profitably; the American Airlines contract, calling for the larger number of commercial transports, was the crucial one.

However, in spite of the merits of the Rainbow and a very successful test programme in 1947, officials at Wright Field became disillusioned as it became obvious that the trend in aviation was towards jet-engined aircraft; furthermore, because of postwar budget cuts, the Air Force decided that it could not afford to operate so highly specialized an aircraft as the XF-12. Thus in mid-1947 the contract for twenty F-12s was cancelled in favour of RB-50s. Simultaneously, American Airlines realized that they would have less passenger revenue than expected, and that the costs of operating the Rainbow would thus be prohibitive. American then cancelled the contract, awarding Republic some compensation since 90 per cent of the tooling needed for production was complete. Shortly thereafter Pan American also backed out since they could not afford to finance the development of an aicraft on their own. Finally, the glut of cheap ex-military transports (some of which were modified by Republic) removed any possibility of other airlines buying the Rainbow.

Republic's decision could now only be to call a halt to plans for producing the aircraft,

and the project was terminated. Eventually one Rainbow crashed following an engine fire (all but one of the crew surviving) and the second was destroyed at the Army's Aberdeen Proving Ground during ordnance tests. Although Republic lost money on the Rainbow project, it was a noble gamble and the company had developed a remarkable aircraft.

The 'Thunderbolt Amphibian'

Ralph Damon departed as President of Republic in 1943 and Alfred Marchev took his place. With the end of the Second World War in sight, Marchev clearly saw the need for Republic to be producing something other than military aircraft and he therefore initiated the Seabee, a civilian amphibian, for what was foreseen as a booming market for private aircraft in the postwar years. Designed to be built quickly and cheaply, the Seabee was one of the most promising designs to emerge from the huge number of personal aircraft in prospect.

The decision to take Republic into the light aircraft market was largely Marchev's, and his enthusiasm carried the Board of Directors along in the autumn of 1943. However, a survey revealed that Republic's offering would have to be something special since few dealers were interested in just another aircraft. Marchev was reminded of a small

amphibian that employee Percival Spencer tried to sell the company in 1941: there was no low-priced amphibian on the market, and Republic considered that they could sell at least 2,500 – the day of the low-cost, mass-produced aircraft had surely arrived and the market was ready to be had been in the same way as the automobile market had been after the First World War. In this belief, Republic wagered three years and several million dollars in an attempt to become the first mass-producer of private aircraft, starting out with the conviction that a four-passenger, all-metal, 100mph amphibian could be so efficiently mass-produced that it could sell for as little as $3,995.

In the late 1930s Percival Spencer had founded the Spencer-Larsen Aircraft Corporation in Amityville, Long Island, for the manufacture of new amphibians, and in 1940 he had developed the 'Amphibian Air Car', which essentially looked like a small, wooden, two-seat Seabee. However, with the outbreak of war, Spencer went to work for nearby Republic as a test pilot, eventually making final check flights on over 130 Lancers and Thunderbolts. In 1943, upon hearing that Republic was interested in entering the civil market, Spencer began a strong promotion of his 'Air Car', promising low cost and utility: with Republic's manufacturing facilities, the company could lead the field. After brief negotiations, the plans and all manufacturing rights were sold to Republic. Spencer was kept on as a design consultant and he delivered the flying prototype to Republic.

While utilizing the basic design of the 'Air Car', Republic quickly decided that their version would be all-metal. By the end of 1943 plans had been drafted and Republic's aircraft had been designated the RC-1 (Republic Commercial 1), originally being named the 'Thunderbolt Amphibian'. By July 1944 the prototype was completed and flying. It performed well but had several flaws that would need correction. Republic's RC-1 was a three-seat, all-metal amphibian with multiple ribs and spars in both the wings and tail, covered with smooth-riveted aluminium sheeting. The aircraft's wing tapered in both plan and front elevation, and the hull had the usual complement of bulkheads and stringers all riveted together. The span was 36ft, the length was 26ft 6in and the aircraft was equipped with a 175hp Franklin engine. The RC-1 was built only to prove the general

design, and conventional structure was used throughout.

During the latter half of 1944 hundreds of hours were spent flight-testing the RC-1 to iron out any possible faults in the design. The major suggestion was that the aircraft should be made into a four-seater: this could be accomplished by eliminating the landing gear retraction housings on both sides of the fuselage and thus allowing the rear seat to expand to the full cabin width. Based on flight performance and projections, by December 1944 thirty distributors had signed up to sell the aircraft on a national basis and soon orders for 1,800 RC-1s were received.

Cutting the costs

However, Republic began to realize that the aircraft would be far more expensive to produce than they had originally anticipated. From the beginning of the Thunderbolt Amphibian project through to the aircraft's first flight, the company had spent $300,000: at that rate, Republic calculated it would cost $1.7 million per year just to build RC-1s, and a very large number of amphibians would have to be sold just to break even. Under the current procedures Republic were looking at a $12,000 amphibian and the Board of Directors wanted a $3,500 aircraft. Marchev quickly set up an investigative team to determine how the aircraft's structures could be simplified in order to reduce manufacturing costs.

The first means of reducing costs was by incorporating as many automobile parts in the airframe as possible, a decision which was to save $1,000 per aircraft. The tapered wing was also abandoned as it was too costly to construct, and Republic's engineers developed a constant-chord, constant-thickness wing having an essentially ribless internal structure, the outer skin having transverse beaded stiffeners to absorb the loads and stresses. When first proposed, this idea created much discussion as doubters questioned the wing's airworthiness because of the absence of ribs, so a complete wing was built and static-tested to 115 per cent of its design load – without causing skin rippling or buckling. The new aircraft was to utilize this full-cantilever wing, braced with single struts and fitted with single-strut floats. Each wing possessed only three ribs and three spars, the theory being that if the cover of a stressed-skin wing was sufficiently stiffened it would carry the loads with a minimum of internal

Left: The original RC-1, with a tapered conventional wing and standard aircraft construction, provided Republic with important, albeit expensive, information regarding the development and production of the Seabee.

structure. Each control surface consisted of a single beaded skin folded upon itself and joined at the trailing edge.

The hull/fuselage became almost a pure monocoque design, of a heavy-gauge, deep-formed, sheet-metal shell with few internal connecting members. It was made of three separate assemblies, spot-welding was employed extensively and only six compartments were needed to ensure complete rigidity and watertightness. Whereas the RC-1 fuselage/hull had 362 parts, the new, simplified design had but 63; the total number of airframe parts was reduced from 1,800 to 450. In sharp contrast to conventional aircraft structure, which contained many small component assemblies put together by hand, the simplified structure of the Republic amphibian lent itself readily to rapid fabrication with equipment of the type used in the automobile industry. Additionally, large sections of the structure could be assembled on automatic riveting machines; for example, in assembling the wing, skin sections were first spliced on an automatic riveting machine to form a large envelope and spars were then

installed progressively, beginning with the front spar, with the riveting again done automatically.

Since the new aircraft, by now named the Seabee, was a four-seater, the retractable landing gear was simplified by designing it to rotate aft and upwards to clear the water. There was a slight penalty in speed but this was more than made up for by eliminating the manufacture of wheel wells and allowing the rear seat to hold two. The cabin was large and comfortable, with interior fittings complementing the latest in automobile design.

The major remaining problem was that of a suitable engine. Republic soon decided on the six-cylinder, air-cooled, 200hp Franklin, but, in 1945, 200hp engines were costing around $1,200 – about one-third of the selling price of the entire aircraft. To get the cost down Republic believed that it would have to achieve the same thriftiness in engine manufacture that it was getting on the airframe, and the only way to do this was to control its own engine company: to this end the company purchased Aircooled Motors (Franklin) of Syracuse, New York, for $1.5

Right: An early production RC-3 Seabee. The Seabee had a rather awkward appearance but a roomy, automobile-like interior. Note the wooden, fixed-pitch propeller.

Left: Casting from the wide bow door opening of the Seabee was a fisherman's dream; the door was also used for docking. Republic hoped that the Seabee would become a popular family leisure aircraft, but its high price was probably the crippling factor.

million. Franklin then became a Republic subsidiary, in a move to integrate Seabee manufacture. For the $740,000 Republic advanced against future orders for engine research, Franklin altered and simplified its 215hp '500' engine so that Republic came to pay $880 a unit instead of the original $1,200; Franklin hoped that it could eventually lower the price to $600.

The Seabee's engine was located above and aft of the cabin for greater safety in landing and docking and to protect the engine from water spray, reduce noise and provide better forward visibility. A bladder-type fuel cell made of rubber-impregnated fabric was located inside the hull between watertight bulkheads. A Koppers ground-adjustable, laminated wooden propeller was standard equipment, the blades being covered with aeroloid plastic sheeting giving them a brown micarta appearance. A Hartzell controllable- and reversible-pitch propeller was optional.

The RC-3 Seabee

By January 1946, with P-47 contracts over, the impetus was placed on a production line of Seabees, now designated RC-3. The aircraft appeared to mark a turning point in the aviation industry – a radical departure from complex, conventional design. Soon a national distribution organization was set up, and with the Seabee's price set at $3,995 (about $500 over the original estimate) Republic was flooded with enquiries. By the spring of 1946 a total of 4,000 Seabees were on order, and Marchev seemed to have been right.

The Seabee had a wing span of 37ft 8in and a length of 28ft. It cruised at 105mph and had a 560-mile range, and it could take off in 800ft from a runway and land in water with only 18in of draught. The cabin was comfortable and roomy, the visibility excellent and the noise level low, and the aircraft was also stable and easy on the controls. By the spring of 1946 RC-3s were rolling off the assembly line. However, during 1946 a national recession struck and the dollar began an upward spiral. Production costs began to rise because of inflation and the increasing costs of materials. By mid-1946 Seabee orders began to be cancelled as Republic was forced to raise the price of the amphibian to $4,495. The whole Seabee project was based on the premise that if the price was low thousands of would-be flyers would buy it, but it soon became obvious that the economic situation that prevailed in 1946 was not as favourable for the sale of private aircraft as had previously been thought. It was decided to continue the manufacture of Seabees for at least a few more months and, in the meantime, to concentrate on a vigorous sales promotion campaign.

In late 1946 Seabees were being produced at a rate of ten aircraft a day. Original proposals called for forty a day, and to that end some $600,000 worth of tools and dies had been ordered from Detroit firms. When these did not arrive on time a check revealed that Republic's orders had been deferred because the manufacturers were using their facilities to fill more lucrative orders from automobile companies. This delay resulted in a nine-month slippage in Seabee production. By mid-1947 the Seabee's unit price had risen to

Left: Like a tadpole with wings, a Seabee soars over the estates and beaches of the once uncluttered Long Island. Note how the landing gear simply swung rearwards in flight. Below left: The view Republic dreamed of – the Seabee as an everyday commuter aircraft. Here a Seabee ties up in lower Manhattan, about 1947. Although Republic lost money on the 1,000 or so aircraft it built, it was a well-constructed machine and many are still flying.

Below: January 1946: three very different Republic aircraft pose on the ramp at Farmingdale. The massive XF-12 dwarfs the famed Thunderbolt, while the RC-1 Seabee offers a very different profile. The XF-12 has still not been painted with national insignia, nor with any other markings.

$6,000 and what market there was appeared to be saturated. By contrast, this same year 90 per cent of all small aircraft were selling for less than $3,500 apiece and many postwar civil aircraft companies were going bankrupt.

The fundamental issue was Republic's traditional problem – poor cash flow. During 1946 the concurrent development costs on the Rainbow, Seabee and P-84 (q.v.) projects proved very steep and ate into Republic's wartime profits. In an effort to save money, administrative and other costs were sharply reduced, with company officers voluntarily accepting reduced salaries. The work force, which had reached a peak of 24,000 in 1944, had fallen to 3,700 in November 1945 and then rose to 6,000 in early 1946. However, by early 1947 Marchev was forced to lay off 3,200 of Republic's 8,000 employees and then issued new stock and secured a $6 million bank loan in an effort to remain solvent. The crisis was the result of a brave attempt by Republic to free itself from complete dependence upon military contracts, and the company's combined operating losses on military and commercial aircraft now amounted to over $4 million. For the aircraft industry in general, 1946 had been a most unsatisfactory year.

Disturbed by corporate losses, Republic's Board of Directors replaced Alfred Marchev as President with Mundy Peale in 1947:

Marchev's gamble in attempting to free Republic from complete reliance on military contracts had cost him his job. For Republic, it now appeared that the future lay in military jets. During 1947 the production requirements of new contracts now pointed to a concentration of all the company's capabilities and facilities on a new jet fighter which had clearly impressed the Air Force. The manufacture of Seabees was discontinued and negotiations were begun to sell the rights to other companies. These negotiations came to naught, however, and Republic decided merely to continue the supply of spare parts and services to the limited degree required.

By late 1947 over 200 Seabees were sitting at Farmingdale awaiting buyers. In early 1948 the final Seabee came off Republic's assembly line after 1,076 had been produced, the last not finding an owner until 1950. No longer having a use for Aircooled Motors, Republic sold the firm to Tucker, which modified the same six-cylinder engine for use in its innovative automobiles.

The Seabee represented a gallant effort to put an extremely flexible aircraft on the market at the lowest possible price through highly original methods of construction. Nonetheless the predicted large postwar civil aircraft market never materialized, and all who entered it lost money.

The Jet Age

THE FIRST NEW American fighter to fly following the end of the Second World War was the jet-powered Republic P-84, the origins of which went back to 1944 during the frenzied American effort to get a jet fighter into production following the appearance of German jets in the skies over Europe. American jet airframe and engine development lagged behind that of Great Britain, and at first, the Air Forces asked Republic to redesign the P-47 around an axial-flow turbojet; the engine would have been installed in the roomy centre fuselage, exhausting under the tail. After the prelimary designs were completed, Kartveli deemed the entire idea impratical and asked that an all-new jet aircraft be created.

USAAF requirements at the time called for a mid-wing day fighter with a top speed of 600mph, a combat radius of 850 miles and an armament of eight M-2 0.50-calibre machine guns. The new aircraft bore no resemblance to the P-47: wanting to obtain the best range and speed from an existing jet engine, Kartveli produced a graceful, highly streamlined design of the utmost simplicity. The new Republic jet had a long, slender fuselage, low, straight wings, a cockpit forward of the wing, tricycle landing gear, no protrusions and flush-riveting throughout. It was designed around one of the earliest American axial-flow turbojet engines, the experimental General Electric TG-180, a more streamlined powerplant than the centrifugal-flow turbojet used in the XP-59 and P-80 and one which required a direct air flow from a nose intake to the engine, via ducting round the cockpit, and out of the tail.

Go-ahead for the P-84

On 11 November 1944 the USAAF accepted Republic's plans and authorized the company to build three XP-84s. There was no competition involving the P-80, P-84 and P-86

Below: December 1945 saw the roll-out of the XP-84, the aircraft devoid of markings. Its extremely clean lines were possible because the airframe was designed around an axial-flow engine.

Right: In 1944 designer Kartveli briefly toyed with the idea of developing a jet-engined P-47 when asked to do so by the Army Air Forces. However, he quickly deemed the whole idea impractical and embarked on the P-84 concept. The jet-powered P-47 would have had its engine buried in its fat fuselage with the exhaust discharging under the tail.

Right: Parked outside Republic's Farmingdale plant, P-84 No. 1 shows how and where the aft fuselage separated for engine maintenance or removal.

since each was significantly better than its predecessor and years apart in development. In February 1945 the full-scale mock-up of the XP-84 was unveiled in Farmingdale. The pressures of war enabled the Republic jet to be completed, dismantled, flown to Muroc (Edwards), California, and reassembled by December 1945, and on 28 February 1946 it made its first flight. The aircraft was powered by a 3,750lb thrust TG-180 (which was soon updated and redesignated the Allison J35-GE-7; it was the first to be powered by an Allison jet engine, and the latter was installed in the first 400 production P-84s, the rear fuselage capable of being detached aft of the wing for easy access. Each landing gear unit collapsed hydraulically to fit into as small a wheel well as possible, in a fashion reminiscent of the P-47.

The second XP-84 was completed in August

that year and on 6 September was flown to a record speed of 611mph, a record enhanced by the fact that it was set by a standard production aircraft, not an experimental model. In 1946 the aircraft was named the Thunderjet by Republic in order to maintain a link with the company's earlier fighter. The Air Force was so pleased with the XP-84 that 25 (later 15) YP-84A Service Test aircraft were ordered as well as 75 (85) production P-84Bs, at a total cost of $17.5 million. The YPs were powered by the Allison J35-A-15, which was essentially identical to the original General Electric model. Provision was made for six 0.50-calibre Colt-Browning M-2 machine guns (the requirement being downgraded from eight), four in the upper fuselage and the remaining two in the wing roots.

Typically for Republic, the company began to experience financial problems at this critical stage of the P-84's development: although it had built over 15,000 P-47s during the war, the cost of developing the new jet fighter ate rapidly into corporate funds. At one bleak point in October 1946 Republic had only enough cash to continue in business for three more weeks. Republic pleaded with the USAAF to begin payments on the P-84 contract, although the first production aircraft would not be delivered for another eight months. After a thorough investigation into the financial standing of the company, Congress and the Air Forces decided to proceed with advance payments, and these payments, plus a fortuitous tax refund of $6 million in 1947, kept Republic and the P-84 alive.

Thunderjets roll

The first production Thunderjets, the P-84Bs, began to reach Air Force units in the summer of 1947. The original contract called for 500 aircraft but only 226 were built, the rest being completed as C and D models. At this time the Air Forces became a fully independent branch of the armed forces and one of its first actions was to change the antiquated aircraft

designation from 'P' (for pursuit) to 'F' (fighter). The P-84B was an improved combat version, equipped with an ejection seat (which was now considered necessary because of the high speed of jet fighters) and also with retractable underwing rocket launchers. As the internal fuel capacity was limited to 415 US gallons, this was supplemented by two streamlined, 230 US gallon auxiliary fuel tanks, carried one on each wing tip. The Bs did have some structural problems, notably fuselage skin wrinkling and wings that needed internal reinforcement, but these were corrected on later models.

Under President Mundy Peale, Republic concentrated on military aircraft and as a result was able to build up production quickly. In the first quarter of 1948 the company showed its first profits since 1945 and the backlog of orders reached $50 million; by the time the Korean War broke out in 1950, Republic would be the largest producer of jet fighters in the Western World. The first Air Force unit to become operational with F-84s was the 14th Fighter Group at Dow Field, Maine, in the summer of 1947.

Below: The P-84 flight-test programme was not without its problems. In early 1947 a YP-84A flown by test pilot Carl Bellinger had an unfortunate accident on Republic's field when the brakes failed upon landing. The aircraft went through a fence, struck several vehicles and flipped over and Bellinger was lucky in that the cockpit came down between two parked cars. He walked away.
Above right: One of the fifteen YP-84A service test aircraft soars over Long Island. For a first attempt at

mating the turbojet engine with a practical airframe, the P-84 was surprisingly successful. The aircraft was equipped with a bubble canopy similar to the P-47's.
Right: The first Thunderjet in service was the P-84B, very similar to the YP-84A but furnished with six machine guns, an ejection seat, a pair of 230-gallon wing-tip fuel tanks and other improvements. Eighty-five were built from June 1947 to February 1948, and by June 1948 the aircraft was redesignated F-84.

As soon as the B model went into mass production at Farmingdale, Kartveli and his engineers began to work on ways to improve the Thunderjet. The 191 F-84Cs featured the Allison J35-A-13C engine and a simplified fuel system, a modified electrical and hydraulic system and a more sophisticated, sequence-controlled bomb-release system. In all, the C weighed a ton more than the B but was considerably improved as a fighter-bomber. The first significant variant in the F-84 programme was the D model: the Air Force had determined that the B and C versions could not meet their intended mission requirements, so the fate of the entire F-84 programme hinged on the new variant. The F-84D was equipped with reinforced wings (so that it could carry heavier ordnance loads), a 'winterized' fuel system and a hinged gun deck cover for the fuselage guns to facilitate re-arming. The D also had fixed (but jettison-able) bomb racks, while small triangular fins were added to the tip tanks to correct a serious stability problem. It was also 700lb heavier than the C, partly accounted for by the improved J35 engine of 5,000lb thrust. The

F-84D proved far superior to earlier Thunderjet models and it was soon to become the standard Air Force fighter-bomber. Some 318 were built, and the aircraft served with Air Force National Guard units until 1957.

F-84Ds were utilized in one bizarre experiment. Project 'Tip Tow' was initiated in 1949, based on German Second World War experiments aimed at greatly extending the ranges of fighters in order to provide effective bomber escorts. The Air Force contracted Republic to modify two F-84Ds in such a way that the aircraft could marry up with the wing tips of an ETB-29A.* The wing tips of all three aircraft were redesigned and the first coupling took place on 21 July 1950; four successful couplings involving all three aircraft had taken place over Long Island by early September. The three aircraft would take off separately and link up in mid-air, the F-84s then throttling back to conserve fuel. The initial test phase was followed by an advanced test phase for which an automatic flight control system was

*Republic's original proposal called for their marrying up with a Rainbow – of course.

Left: The F-84D was the first really significant variant in the Thunderjet programme. It featured a more powerful engine and a strengthened airframe as well as other improvements. It was the first F-84 model to be deployed outside the United States.
Below left: In 1949 Project 'Tip Tow' was initiated in an attempt to enable fighters to extend their coverage of bombers all the way to their targets. Under this scheme two F-84s were to hook up to the wings of a B-29 in flight.

Above right: Many successful hook-ups were made involving an ETB-29A and a pair of F-84Ds between 1950 and 1953. However, a disastrous crash in 1953 terminated the programme. Once connected, the F-84s would have throttled back to conserve fuel.
Right: The complicated wing-tip connections on the B-29 and F-84D generally worked well through many tests.

installed on the F-84s so that their pilots would not have to work once coupled to the B-29; six such flights were successfully made in the spring of 1953. However, on 24 April 1953 the port-side F-84D ran into major problems with its automatic control system while coupled and it subsequently flipped up on to the mother-ship's wing without warning; both aircraft broke apart and crashed into Peconic Bay, killing all the crewmen. Project 'Tip Tow' was brought to an end, although the basic premise remained and would be resurrected.

What appeared to be the final version of the Thunderjet was the F-84E. This airframe was strengthened to take a pair of stores pylons on the wing roots, allowing it to carry two 1,000lb bombs or two 230 US gallon drop tanks. It also incorporated a Sperry A-1B radar-directed gun sight and a stretched fuselage to accom-

modate the 5,000lb thrust J35-A-17D engine and for added pilot comfort. The E could reach 613mph at sea level and had a larger internal fuel capacity, giving it a ferry range of 2,000 miles. Maintenance was also improved through the adoption of electrical quick-disconnects and extra access covers. In all, 843 F-84Es were built, of which 100 went to NATO countries, principally France. This seemed to be the end of the line for the straight-wing jet: with increased power the speed limitations of the airframe had been reached.

The F-96

Concerned about the success of the F-86 Sabre, Kartveli began preliminary design work on a high-speed, swept-wing version of the F-84 as early as the spring of 1947, and, after unsuccessful attempts to sell this aircraft to

Above: With the appearance of the F-84E, Republic had produced a fighter-bomber with an unmatched speed, range and load-carrying capability. It featured a more powerful engine and a lengthened fuselage, and the internal fuel capacity was increased; an additional pair of 230-gallon tanks could be carried beneath the wing.
Below: This head-on photograph of an F-84E illustrates one of the numerous ordnance combinations which the Thunderjet could carry: thirty-two 5in high-velocity rockets are hung from every available hardpoint.

Above: By the time of the Korean War both Republic and the Air Force realized that the straight-winged F-84 design had progressed about as far as it could. Thus in order to improve performance further an F-84E was modified with swept wings and a new tail; it was originally designated YF-96A. Below: The YF-96A (F-84F prototype) featured an F-84E fuselage, a circular intake, an old-style sliding canopy and an unusual vee-shaped windscreen.

the Air Force, Republic, not wishing to be left behind in the technology race, decided to develop the swept-wing Thunderjet as an in-house project. In all, the company spent $2 million of corporate funds developing it. In November 1949 Republic again submitted its swept-wing F-84 proposal to the Air Force, as design AP-23M; its main characteristics were a swept wing of increased area, swept tail sur-faces, provision for carrying 8,000lb of ordnance and an estimated top speed of 730mph. This time the Air Force was quick to support the idea, and it issued a contract in February 1950 for the new jet, now designated YF-96A. The project was given priority by both the Air Force and Republic and the roll-out of the first completed aircraft was scheduled for May.

One of the snags with earlier F-84s was that the Allison J35 engine was still in the 5,000lb thrust range although the aircraft's loaded weight had risen dramatically through several versions; the F-84 was, furthermore, such a tight, streamlined design that there was now no room for a larger, more powerful engine. However, Republic did the best it could, and the 209th F-84E was diverted to serve as the development airframe for the YF-96A. Its fuselage was mated with new 40-degree swept wings and swept tail surfaces (although it still incorporated the 5,200lb thrust J35) and a long, more streamlined cockpit completed the changes. The new fighter first flew on 3 June 1950, only 167 days after the first engineering work began. At this point almost 60 per cent of the airframe was derived from the F-84E. Republic was still unhappy with the aircraft's powerplant and the search continued for a

more suitable engine. At first plans were drawn up around a new 5,800lb thrust version of the J35 known as the A-29, but this engine too proved to have insufficient power. Fortunately, however, at the same time, Curtiss-Wright acquired the licence to produce the 7,200lb thrust Armstrong-Siddeley Sapphire (US designation J65) and in October 1950 Republic selected this engine to power the F-96A.

The J65, however, consumed a greater volume of air than the J35, and it was therefore necessary to modify the fuselage of the new aircraft by deepening it some 7in, imparting a more oval cross-section; the air intake was similarly changed. The wings were strengthened, heavier landing gear was fitted and perforated air brakes and a rising canopy were installed, creating, in effect, an entirely new machine. Flight-testing with the first YF-96A revealed ineffective ailerons and speed brakes, an inadequate windshield and a lower than expected cruising altitude and range. All these problems could be solved, but with the

outbreak of the Korean War the Air Force needed new aircraft immediately and therefore asked Republic to develop and build an interim design while the YF-96's problems were being solved.

The F-84G

Republic decided that the straight-wing Thunderjet did have some potential for improvement and they directed their efforts at giving it longer range. An air-to-air refuelling capability was insisted upon by the Air Force as the latter still intended the F-84 to function primarily as a bomber escort; the system would also be required for the long-range, high-speed delivery of nuclear weapons. This was the first time a fighter had provision for refuelling in flight, a hardpoint receptacle being installed in the port wing for accepting fuel via the flying boom system. The equipment was so designed that incoming fuel was distributed to all the tanks at the same time, in order to keep the aircraft in trim, and a single transfer took 2.5min. The new

Thunderjet, the F-84G, was also given a reinforced cross-braced canopy and, to ease pilot fatigue on long-distance flights, an autopilot. Although both the Air Force and Republic intended the F-84G to be an interim aircraft until the swept-wing Thunderjet came on line, delays encountered in that programme, combined with the needs of the Korean War, meant that the G was produced in greater numbers than any other F-84 model. A total of 3,025 F-84Gs were built, 1,936 of these serving with twelve foreign air forces, mostly of NATO countries.

Like earlier F-84s, the G was armed with six 0.50-calibre M-3 machine guns and had eight hard points for external stores comprising bombs, rockets, napalm or additional fuel tanks. It was the first single-seat aircraft capable of carrying an atomic bomb and, thanks to air-to-air refuelling, the first fighter able to fly the Atlantic and Pacific non-stop. Power was provided by a 5,600lb thrust Allison J35-A-29 engine; in addition, two rocket assisted take-off (RATO) units could be attached to the underside of the fuselage in order to reduce the take-off run and enable the aircraft to carry heavier loads than otherwise possible. The top speed was 622mph at sea level and the service ceiling 40,000ft; unrefuelled range was 2,000 miles. Wing span was 36ft 5in, length 38ft and empty weight 11,095lb. F-84Gs first became operational in August 1951, and in the summer of 1952 the first units were sent to Korea. On 18 May 1955 four F-84Gs set a new world non-stop distance record for fighters, flying from Yokota Air Base in Japan to Newcastle in Australia. Thunderjets were also used on a

Far left: F-84Gs under assembly at Farmingdale.

Left: An idea that cropped up during the 1950s involved spotting aircraft about the countryside in specially designed concrete shelters, to be launched should a nuclear attack be made by the enemy. A number of Thunderjets were reworked for tests of this system, being kicked into the air by a powerful solid-fuel booster rocket and thus eliminating the need for a conventional runway. Right: 'The Thunderbirds', the US Air Force's aerobatic team, flew F-84Gs from its inception in 1953 until they were phased out in favour of F-84Fs in 1955.

public relations tour of Europe by the aerobatic team of the 36th Fighter Bomber Wing, 'The Skyblazers', in 1951–52 (they also gave one air display at Republic's factory), and the US Air Force's aerobatic team, 'The Thunderbirds', flew F-84Gs from 1953 to 1955.

The Thunderjet at war

In June 1950 North Korean troops moved into South Korea and the Korean War began. At first, the Air Force believed that the F-51s and F-82s in Korea would be adequate to deal with whatever ex-Soviet aircraft the North Koreans could field, but in November 1950 Soviet-built MiG-15 jets first rose from airfields in North Korea and, in response, Fifth Air Force generals ordered the F-84 and F-86 into combat. In the summer of 1950, just weeks after the war began, the Air Force had announced a $200 million order for new Thunderjets. Republic's workforce rose

quickly from 6,000 to 8,000, and to 15,000 by the year's end. Sales rose to $130 million by late 1950, the company posted a $2.3 million net profit and there was a backlog of $245 million in orders. The F-84 proved to be the best fighter-bomber of the Korean War and it set impressive records for the number of missions flown.

The 27th Fighter-Escort Wing, flying F-84Ds, became the first operational Thunderjet unit, beginning missions on 6 December 1950. Their first operational sortie was led by Lt. Col. Don Blakeslee, who had also led the first P-47s into combat over Europe. At first the F-84s operated from steel mats at Taegu and Itazuke airfields, all maintenance being done in the open, often in freezing weather. Originally the Thunderjets were assigned to escort lumbering B-29s on bombing missions. However, in this role they proved less than successful as the MiG-15s they often ran into proved faster, more manoeuvrable and better armed. The F-84 was clearly not the equal of the MiG-15, but superior pilot training allowed it to hold its own. The F-84s gave up the escort role to the more suitable F-86s, and they then concentrated on ground-attack operations, contributing immensely to an interdiction campaign which virtually cut off North Korean forces fighting in the South.

Early in 1951 the 27th Wing was joined by the 136th Air National Guard Wing flying F-84Es, concentrating at first on the close support of retreating UN forces; it was during this period, on 22 January 1951, that a Thunderjet pilot recorded the first MiG-15 'kill' by an F-84. During 1951 all the F-84s in Korea were assigned to Operation 'Strangle', aimed at preventing the communists from moving supplies and reinforcements down from China to the Front. At the time the F-84s could carry the largest ordnance loads of any fighter-bomber then available. They were armed with 1,800 rounds of 0.50-calibre ammunition, a combination of 5in HVAR or 2.75in aircraft rockets, two 1,200lb 'Tiny Tim' rockets and up to 1,000lb of bombs and napalm, the last proving very effective against enemy troops and transport. Carrying this array of ordnance, F-84s roamed behind enemy lines destroying whatever targets of opportunity they found – tanks, trucks, bridges, trains and troop concentrations. So successful was Operation 'Strangle' that soon large numbers of MiG-15s appeared, trying to break up the Thunderjet formations.

Left: Combat-ready F-84s of the 9th FBS sit on the ramp in Taegu, February 1952. Maintenance of F-84s in Korea was performed mostly in the open – often in harsh weather.

Frank Everest, Commander of the Fifth Air Force, called the F-84 'the backbone of the concentrated interdiction program pursued by the 5th Air Force in Korea'. He went on: 'Through these systematic low-level attacks, they are helping to deny the enemy the opportunity to prepare for an offensive while engaging in ceasefire parleys at Panmunjom. Thunderjets have hit targets all over North Korea with bombs, rockets, machine-gun fire and napalm, inflicting a heavy toll. Chinese communists dread the sight of our Thunderjets.'

F-84Gs rolled off Republic's assembly lines all through the conflict, and Thunderjets were involved in every major air operation during the final two and a half years of the war. They proved to be able to take a fair amount of ground fire and keep flying, and they were comparatively easy to maintain. F-84s led the great dam raids in the summer of 1952, which resulted in the loss of all electrical power to North Korea, as well as two spectacular raids on irrigation dams at Tokson and Chusan in May 1953. The final tally for F-84s in Korea was 86,408 missions flown, 50,427 tons of bombs dropped, 5,560 tons of napalm delivered and, in spite of the Republic aircraft's handicap in dogfighting, 105 MiG-15s destroyed or damaged. In turn, eighteen F-84s were shot down by MiGs and a further 155 by anti-aircraft fire. F-84s destroyed 200,807 buildings, 3,317 vehicles, 10,673 rail cuts, 3,996 railway wagons, 4,846 gun positions, 167 tanks, 259 locomotives and 588 bridges.

The F-84F Thunderstreak

Shortly after the YF-96A made its first flight in June 1950 its designation was changed to F-84F. It was significantly different enough to warrant a new designation, and in fact Republic wanted to call it the F-96, but at the time the Air Force was having difficulty securing funds from Congress for a new aircraft and found it much easier to get funding simply to continue an existing programme. Through this skulduggery, the F-84 designation was retained, even though the 'F model' was virtually a brand new aircraft. The first two prototype Fs had sliding canopies, as on the E, and vee-shaped windscreens; production aircraft were given a flat-plate windscreen and a rising clamshell canopy that was retained on the XF-91.

As related, the first two YF-84Fs were powered by 7,200lb thrust Armstrong-Siddeley Sapphires, produced in America as Curtiss-Wright J65-W-1s. The first YF-84F set the shape of all subsequent F-84Fs, but the second aircraft was modified with a streamlined, solid nose and wing-root air intakes, in order to investigate the effects of the latter; the aircraft first flew in this form on

Below: A new F-84F gets its final check at Republic's plant. The oval intake was required to capture more air for the J65 engine, and the extraordinarily wide track of the main landing gear made the aircraft very stable on the ground. Note the upward-rising clamshell canopy.

14 February 1951. These experimental split intakes were flawed in design and reduced the air flow to the engine, and they were not, therefore, considered for production F-84F fighters. However, the second YF-84F was eventually to serve as the prototype for the reconnaissance RF-84F.

The production F-84F, which first flew on 22 November 1952, was far superior to the straight-wing F-84, and by this stage only 15 per cent of the tooling was interchangeable. The wings were of rib and spar construction with conventional ailerons, spoilers and partial span flaps; early machines had leading-edge slats. All the flight controls were hydraulically operated, with a mechanical back-up. The conventional fin and rudder were retained throughout the production run but the horizontal stabilizers and elevators were, after the first 275 aircraft, deleted in

favour of a one-piece flying tail (stabilator) to improve the poor lateral stability. There was a 16ft braking parachute to shorten the landing run. The tricycle undercarriage was fully retractable, the main gear being accommodated in wells in the wing and lower fuselage. All the fuel tanks – forward, wing, main and pylon – could be replenished via a single conventional receiver on the upper surface of the port wing.

An AN/APW-11 radar set was standard equipment, as was an AN/ARN-6 radio compass, a Lear F-5 autopilot, an A-4 gun sight and an MA-2 LABS (Low Altitude Bombing System) computer. The armament was the same as for the F-84E – six 0.50-calibre M-3 machine guns, four in the nose and one in each wing root. Four underwing pylons could carry 2.75in rockets, CBU-1 and CBU-2 cluster bombs, BLU fire bombs, MLU-10B land mine

units, two dozen 5in HVAR, 2,000lb bombs or two 425 US gallon auxiliary fuel tanks. The total ordnance load was a maximum of three tons, to accommodate which Republic gave the F-84F a RATO capability consisting of four 14-AS-100 bottles mounted on the fuselage's

underside. The Thunderstreak could also carry a single Mk 6 nuclear device under the port wing. This would be accurately placed by the LAB computer, the release being effected when the aircraft was rolling up in a loop to enable the pilot to get clear of the blast.

The Thunderstreak had a length of 43ft 4in, a wing span of 33ft 6in and a maximum speed of 690mph; its service ceiling was 45,000ft and its range of 1,500 miles could be extended indefinitely with air-to-air refuelling. Some F-84s could also carry a buddy tank in order to refuel other fighters in flight. The first 275 aircraft were powered by 7,200lb thrust Curtiss-Wright J65-3 engines, the remainder by Buick-built J65-W-7s of 7,800lb. Unfortunately, during 1953 and 1954 serious problems were encountered delivering these powerplants, forcing Republic to store up to 450 completed F-84Fs at company premises, postponing aircraft deliveries by one year and causing 7,000 of their 29,000 employees – the latter the

Far left: By the time F-84F No. 267 had been reached the aircraft incorporated a one-piece flying tailplane for better stability. All subsequent F-84s were to show this new feature.
Below: Acceleration using RATO bottles was exceptional. However, they could not be turned off and once they were ignited the pilot was committed to take-off.

Left: Operational F-84Fs were usually flown with wing-mounted drop tanks in place, as on these two 27th SFW aircraft.

Right: The F-84F could carry a wide variety of ordnance. This aircraft has twenty-four 5in HVARs (air-to-surface missiles), hung from every available pylon. To take this load into the air the aircraft is equipped with four RATO bottles.

highest figure ever for the company – to be laid off.

Not only the US Air Force was ordering the F-84F. Many were being sent to European countries as well, and to meet the demand a second assembly line was required. This was established at a General Motors factory in Kansas City, although Republic was unhappy with the decision as it had no say in the selection. However, a total of 599 F-84Fs were built in Kansas City, out of a grand total of 2,711. Production ended in 1957.

Below: F-84F final assembly in Republic's Building 17 in 1954; note the forward hinged gun bay. Over fifty aircraft are visible.

The first unit to be equipped with the F-84F was the 506th Strategic Fighter Wing at Dow AFB, Maine, in January 1954, and by 1955 twelve Air Force Wings were operating the type. In 1957 all F-84Fs were transferred to Tactical Air Command. NATO began to arm with the Thunderstreak in 1955 and eventually the aircraft served with the air forces of France, Belgium, Holland, Italy, West Germany, Greece and Turkey. The only F-84Fs to see combat were those flown by the French Air Force, which saw action against Egypt during the Suez crisis of 1956. In March 1955 an F-84F piloted by Lt. Col. Robert Scott set a transcontinental speed record, flying from Los Angeles to New York in 3hr 44min. Thunderstreaks also served with the USAF 'Thunderbirds' aerobatic team in 1955–56 and the last unit to operate the type was the Illinois Air Guard, which finally exchanged its aircraft in 1971.

Concurrent with the development of the F-84F, in 1951 Republic inaugurated a unique and effective engineer recruitment programme. For several years the American aviation industry had been engaged in fierce competition because of a sharp decrease in

Above: In 1955–56 'The Thunderbirds' flew F-84Fs, performing at 91 air shows. The only modifications to the aircraft comprised the addition of a smoke system and special communications equipment.

Below and above right: Refuelling the F-84F in flight involved the use of the 'flying boom' system. The refuelling receptacle was mounted in the port wing root, but the pilot's ability to monitor the operation was limited by the fact that the

receptacle was located behind his convenient field of view.
Right: This Thunderstreak carries a mix of 500lb bombs and HVARs. The four RATO bottles, mounted on a large bracket assembly, are plainly visible.

Left: Republic also developed its own a 'buddy' refuelling system utilizing the probe and drogue system, the drogue and fuel being carried in the port drop tank and deployed via a mechanical arm. Here an F-84F refuels a Navy F9F Cougar. The system was never operational.

the number of engineers graduating each year since the end of the Second World War. Vast advertising campaigns were put into operation, and all sorts of inducements were offered. Republic devised an ingenious scheme. Surveys revealed that there were large numbers of engineers living in New York City, its northern suburbs, Connecticut and New Jersey who would work for Republic but did not wish to move to Long Island nor commute all the way to Farmingdale. The company therefore leased 40,000 square feet of space in the Dunn & Bradstreet building in Lower Manhattan, and some 400 engineers – a remarkable number for the times – were recruited in this way.

Ringed in by security systems as these new Republic offices were, few of the neighbours could know that some of the nation's most advanced fighter aircraft were gradually taking shape in a district otherwise devoted to high finance. They would also have been aston-

ished to discover that a mock-up and a good part of the prototype of the top-secret F-105 were actually being assembled in a seemingly vacant loft in downtown Manhattan, to be spirited out to Farmingdale at night in enclosed vans. By the end of 1954 some 90 per cent of the New York City engineers had been persuaded to move to Long Island.

The RF-84F Thunderflash

In 1949 Republic proposed a swept-wing reconnaissance version of the F-84E, but this was not taken up by the Air Force. However, as a direct result of the Korean War, the USAF saw the need for a new high-speed photo-reconnaissance aircraft that could deal with the MiG-15 as an equal if engaged. Thus Republic built a new version of the second YF-84F, modifying its forward fuselage to house six cameras and assorted electrical equipment. The Air Force awarded the company a contract for the new aircraft in April

Left: In an effort to extend the life of the F-84F, an airframe was modified with a deeper fuselage to take the 8,920lb thrust GE YJ73 engine. This YF-84J was first flown in May 1954 although the increase in performance did not warrant production and the project was abandoned in favour of the F-105.

Above: Once engine deliveries began again, F-84Fs were first run up and tested using special mufflers to dampen the noise as local residents were increasingly complaining about the din.

Right: The first production RF-84F differed considerably from the prototype: the wing root intakes were wider, it featured an upward-rising canopy and the nose was configured to hold an assortment of cameras.

Below: The main instrument panel of an F-84F, showing more switches and dials than that of the P-47. This early-model panel features the original gunsight which adversely affected the forward vision of the pilot.

1951 and the YRF-84F first flew in the hands of test pilot Carl Bellinger in February 1952. Unlike most previous reconnaissance aircraft, the RF-84F, now named the Thunderflash, was armed with four 0.50-calibre machine guns installed in the intake walls. As the ducting problems had been solved in the second YF-84F, this aircraft was the sole pre-production RF variant and it led to the first order, for 130 RF-84Fs, in 1951.

The RF-84F had essentially the same performance as the F-84F but the airframe modifications reduced speed marginally and increased weight. From the start the Thunderflash incorporated a one-piece flying tailplane as used in later Thunderstreaks. The two intake ducts were located in the wing

roots, the wing chord being extended forward to encompass the new structure; boundary layer fences were added to the outer wings. The Thunderflash was the first operational reconnaissance aircraft to carry a full range of cameras – including dicing cameras for close-up photographs of individual targets and tri-metrogen cameras for horizon-to-horizon shots – and had a day/night capability thanks to its special night cameras and underwing magnesium flare ejectors. In all, some fifteen cameras could be carried in the extended nose, allowing the RF-84F to undertake any reconnaissance task. The pilot was also given a visual viewfinder, its display screen mounted in the instrument panel, and a computer-operated camera control system.

The RF-84F had a wing span of 33ft 6in and a length of 47ft 6in; its top speed was 650mph and its ceiling 37,000ft. It also was powered by the J65-W-3. The Thunderflash became operational with the US Air Force in March 1954 and it served with both Strategic Air Command and Tactical Air Command. A total of 715 RF-84Fs were built between 1952 and

Left: RF-84F final assembly in Republic's Building 29C, 1956.
Below left: The last production RF-84F was pulled from Republic's final assembly building in December 1957. This was the 716th Thunderflash to be built.
Right: Republic's main plant in 1957, showing new F-84Fs, an RF-84F and an RF-84K.
Below: The YRF-84F prototype at Edwards AFB, July 1952. The aircraft featured a reinforced F-84G-style canopy but, being primarily an aerodynamic prototype to test the split intakes, was not equipped with nose-mounted cameras.

1958, 386 being supplied to Belgium, Denmark, France, West Germany, Greece, Italy, the Netherlands, Norway, Turkey and Taiwan and serving with several of these countries' air forces until the late 1970s.

In the mid-1950s the US Air Force initiated Project 'Tom Tom', similar to the unsuccessful Project 'Tip Tow' several years earlier. In an effort to increase the range of the Thunderflash, two RF-84Fs and a KRB-36F

Left: The Thunderflash could house up to six cameras in its enlarged nose although a much wider variety of cameras was available for use.

Below: In 1955 the RF-84K made its appearance. This was a standard RF-84F reconfigured, under the FICON programme, to make an in-flight hook-up with a GRB-36. Modifications to the RF-84F included a retractable nose hook and a stabilator with 23 degrees of anhedral to allow it to fit in the bomb bay of the B-36.

were modified with wing-tip jaws and clamps so all could join in mid-air. The first successful link-up occurred on 24 April 1956 and fifty more were made. The major problem encountered was aerodynamic and not mechanical: the comparatively small RF-84Fs were adversely affected by the tip vortices put out by the KRB-36F's massive wings. The last link-up took place on 26 September 1956 and almost ended in the same way as 'Tip Tow': one RF-84F began to vibrate wildly because of incorrect latching and shortly thereafter the latch mechanism failed altogether. Both aircraft suffered damaged wings, but both landed safely. The Air Force decided to end the programme, especially since the FICON project was proving much more successful.

In 1954 Republic produced two YF-84Js (modified from F-84Fs), powered by General Electric YJ73-GE-7 engines of 8,920lb thrust – over twice that of the prototype F-84. The model had a deepened fuselage and a reconfigured nose intake with a raked upper lip. However, the gain in performance proved marginal and the Air Force decided not to proceed with production.

FICON

The FICON (Fighter Conveyor) programme was one of the most interesting applications of the RF-84F. The concept of bombers carrying their own fighter escort was revived with the huge, seemingly vulnerable B-36. The idea was to develop an ultra-long-range fighter, atomic bomber, or swift reconnaissance aircraft and the RF-84F was the only aircraft qualified. A B-36 was modified to carry a trapeze recovery system in the bomb bay, and the first tests were initiated with an F-84E at Edwards Air Force Base in 1952; shortly thereafter all testing was carried out using the modified YF-84F prototype. Early trials proved successful, and it was decided to proceed with an expanded programme. Both aircraft would take off separately and rendezvous in mid-air, and a trapeze would be lowered from the GRB-36 which engaged and hoisted the fighter into the mother-ship's bomb bay with its wings and horizontal stabilizer protruding. With a range of 10,000 miles for the B-36 plus 2,000 miles for the RF-84F, any point on Earth could be covered from bases in the United States.

Following successful tests in 1954 and 1955, twenty-five RF-84Fs were modified into RF-84Ks for the FICON mission. The modifications consisted of downward-drooping stabilizers (23-degree anhedral) to permit stowage in the B-36 and a large, articulated, retractable hydraulic hook on the upper fuselage in front of the windscreen. (It transpired that the drooping tail improved lateral control signifi-

Left: The first tests for the FICON programme were made in 1952 with the suitably modified YF-84F. These trials were successful and led to the RF-84K. Total range of the system was 12,000 miles non-refuelled.

Left: The GRB-36 trapeze assembly was raised and lowered hydraulically; the bomb bay doors were removed and the trapeze was offset to one side to allow for canopy clearance. The pilot would enter the RF-84K from inside the B-36 and the bomber took off and landed with the RF-84K attached (in contrast to the arrangements for Projects 'Tip Tow' and 'Tom Tom').

cantly, and for a while the Air Force considered retrofitting all F-84Fs in such a manner.) FICON and the RF-84Ks were deployed operationally in 1955 with the 71st Strategic Reconnaissance Wing, but within a short time the programme was terminated, owing in large part to the advent of the B-52.

The F-84H

Probably the strangest, and most spectacular, version of the F-84 was that developed for the US Navy in the early 1950s. In 1951 the Navy was seeking a turboprop-driven fighter with jet-type performance for operation from aircraft carriers. In response, Republic proposed its Model AP-46, a radically modified RF-84F, with the nose redesigned to take a 5,850hp Allison XT40-A-1. A contract was issued for three aircraft, two going to the Air Force to test the concepts of a turboprop fighter as well as that of the supersonic propeller. The aircraft were originally designated XF-106 but shortly thereafter this was changed to XF-84H – despite which it had little in common with the Thunderstreak.

The XF-84H was to offer the combined advantages of propeller-driven aircraft (for example, quick acceleration) with those of the jet (i.e., sustained high speed). Thus the aircraft would be able to take off with heavy loads from a short runway, or from an aircraft carrier. There were several major differences between the XF-84H and the Thunderstreak. The H model had a high, T-shaped tail and an anti-torque fin ('vortex gate') on top of the fuselage behind the cockpit to neutralize the torque set up by the powerful propeller. Thrust came from the Allison XT40, driving a stubby, three-bladed, 12ft-diameter Aero-products D-91 supersonic propeller with a large spinner, the power of the turbine engine being converted through a gearbox and shafting. An automatic governor controlled the XT-40's rpm in order to maintain a constant speed; the throttle simply changed the pitch of the propeller to provide the needed thrust. The propeller, which could be reversed on the ground for braking, caused a unique and

unexpected problem during the testing programme. During ground run-ups, the thin, supersonic blades created sound waves which, although inaudible to the human ear, caused acute nausea in anyone standing within several hundred feet of the aircraft. Difficulties with the brakes and engine gearbox and various hydraulic leaks delayed the first flight until 22 July 1955, when the XF-84H reached over 20,000ft.

Flight testing the XF-84H was limited, but the aircraft's handling characteristics were reported as very good and it was said to have reached a top speed of 670mph, making it the fastest propeller-driven aircraft to date. The second XF-84H was completed but never flown and the third, with an afterburning engine, was never built. The XT40 engine, also intended to be used in the Douglas XA2D Skyshark, proved too troublesome to warrant

Below: Twenty-five RF-84Ks were built and all were assigned to the 91st SRS. The unit markings were minimal.

further investigation and trials ended in 1956 because of persistent problems with it and with propeller vibration; moreover, the advent of the angled deck and the development of steam catapults on board carriers rendered the concept obsolete.

The XF-84H had the same wing span as the Thunderstreak – 33ft 6in – but its length was 51ft 4in. Its ceiling was 40,000ft and it had an estimated range of 2,000 miles, and it was also designed to carry up to 4,000lb of bombs as well as a single 0.60-calibre machine gun. It was the last complete propeller-driven aircraft built by Republic, although the company did propose two developed versions of the F-84F in an effort to extend the programme. One was a high-speed, twin-engined version, with a streamlined, pointed nose; the other was the vertical take-off F-84VF, with lift thrust directed through the wing roots. Neither project was accepted by the Air Force and eventually the Thunderstreak was replaced by the F-100 Super Sabre and F-101 Voodoo. In all, 7,883 F-84s were constructed, of which 4,457 had straight wings.

The XF-91 Thunderceptor

The rocket engine as a mode of propulsion had interested aircraft designers for a long time. The German Messerschmitt Me 163 Komet was the world's first rocket fighter but its eight-minute endurance in powered flight severely limited its use; nonetheless, the idea of rocket power to push a fighter past the speed of sound still appealed to aircraft engineers – and led to the development of the Republic XF-91, one of the most unusual aircraft ever to fly. Unfortunately, however, despite the ingenuity of its designers, the aircraft was a product of the late 1940s and was thus supplanted by creations of the 1950s, such as the Convair F-102, which were better able to perform it original mission.

In 1946, in response to an Air Force Request for Proposals, Kartveli and Republic proposed a new jet-powered, high-altitude interceptor capable of meeting and destroying enemy (i.e., Soviet) nuclear bombers and with the unprecedented ability to exceed Mach 1 in level flight. At the time, both jet engines and swept wings were radically new, but, although this was Republic's first swept-wing aircraft, the company was not hesitant about incorporating these and a number of other advanced features. Thus the XF-91 was proposed at a time when little was known

Above: The world's fastest propeller-driven aircraft to date is the Republic XF-84H. Seen here on the company's ramp prior to shipment to Edwards AFB, XF-84H No. 1 reveals its major design changes – a high 'T' tail, an anti-torque fin behind the cockpit and a massive turboprop propeller. The 'T' tail was needed to allow the pitch control surface to operate in air flow unaffected by propeller wash.
Left: The XF-84H first flew in July 1955 and the noise put out by its XT40 engine and supersonic propeller proved overpowering. The aircraft combined the quick acceleration and fuel efficiency of a propeller-driven machine with the high cruise speed of a jet. The Navy had some interest in the project but the advent of steam catapults and angled decks made the aircraft obsolete.

F-84F/V

Above left: F-84s that never were. Among proposed versions in the mid-1960s were a twin-engined version powered by GE1/J1Bs and a four-engined variant powered by GE J85s and designed for close air support with a combat range of 200 miles.
Above: Another F-84F design incorporated a VTOL capability. This version would have featured wing-mounted lift/cruise engines. Nothing came of the proposal.
Left: The XF-91 Thunderceptor is rolled out at Republic's Farmingdale plant. Note the unusual tandem-wheel main landing gear, the open main gear door hanging down near the wing tip, the fully deployed speed brake beneath the centre fuselage and the massive, 541-gallon drop tanks.

about the territory beyond Mach 1; indeed, it flew just two years after Chuck Yeager had broken the sound barrier. Republic's proposal was accepted by the Air Force, and a contract worth $10 million was placed for two aircraft originally designated XP-91. The new aircraft would fulfil the same role as the Me 163 – that of a daytime target defence interceptor.

It was soon determined, however, that the 5,200lb thrust of the General Electric J47 turbojet, the intended engine for the XP-91, would be inadequate if supersonic speeds in level flight were to be achieved; this was a problem that was to afflict most early turbojet aircraft. The performance requirements of speed and range therefore imposed a unique approach to the XP-91's propulsion system, and the decision was taken to augment the afterburning turbojet with a rocket motor to achieve the desired thrust. This combination was to give a very fast rate of climb and a maximum endurance of two hours at cruising speed (though obviously less in combat). The XF-91 became the first American mixed-power combat-type aircraft, and the only American 'rocket fighter'.

The rocket motor was originally to have been the Curtiss-Wright XLR27: larger and more powerful than any other such engine then available for aircraft use, this was a four-chamber unit with a total thrust of 13,000lb. Unfortunately, the manufacturer was never able to get the XLR27 to perform properly during tests, possibly because of the stringent safety requirements imposed by the Air Force, and, rather than delay the entire programme Republic decided that the motor would have to be changed.

Reaction Motors Industries' four-chamber XLR11 rocket engine, with a total thrust of 6,000lb, was then chosen as a smaller but adequate (and available) unit in order to get the aircraft flying; it had already proven its reliability as it had been used in the supersonic Bell X-1. The XLR27 rocket chambers were originally positioned in vertical pairs in fairings above and below the afterburner tube, but with the switch to the XLR11 the lower fairing was enlarged to hold all four chambers in a diamond pattern. The available thrust for the XF-91 would be more than doubled once the rocket motors were cut in, and this combination of jet and rocket propulsion would give the aircraft a performance higher than that of any other fighter in the world.

On 24 February 1949 Republic rolled out the XF-91, the company's first swept-wing aircraft, now called the Thunderceptor. It featured some astonishing innovations, and the rocket engines were not the most unusual. Because of Kartveli's streamlining, the lines of the fuselage were somewhat similar to those of the earlier F-84s', but the similarity stopped there. The Thunderceptor's 35-degree swept-back wing could be adjusted in flight to vary the incidence from −2 to +6 degrees so as to create the most efficient angles for take-off, cruise and landing. It could also be adjusted quickly in flight, to increase the aircraft's combat manoeuvrability by creating sudden increases in lift, causing the aircraft to 'jump' without changing pitch and making it a much more difficult target to hit. However, despite Republic's efforts (and similar work undertaken by other manufacturers at the time), this interesting feature was never incorporated in any fighter and only today are advanced jet fighters being developed with canards to give them this kind of agility. The

XF-91 also featured full-span leading-edge slats, enabling it to fly at lower speeds than any other fighter of its time.

By far the most peculiar feature of the XF-91, however, was its inversely tapered wing, with the thickest and widest part at its tip (12ft 10in chord) instead of its root (7ft 11in chord). This layout provided greater lift outboard and reduced the tendency of the wing tips to stall at low speeds. Wing-tip stall was an alarming problem in early swept-wing aircraft. With a normal swept-wing jet, stall occurs first at the tips, pitching the nose up and thus worsening the stall. The XF-91's wing reversed this tendency, pitching the nose down and promoting swift recovery, and it also reduced drag at the critical wing/fuselage junction. The problem of accommodating the main landing gear was met by an obvious but unorthodox solution whereby it was simply retracted outward to fit into the thicker wing tips, a tandem-wheel arrangement under each wing being adopted to permit smaller-diameter wheels to be used. This arrangement also

Right: An overhead view of the XF-91 reveals the vee-shaped windscreen and the extremely thin, tandem-wheel main gear. The inversely tapered wing, the aircraft's most remarkable feature, also incorporated variable incidence, providing a lower angle of attack for high-speed flight and a higher angle for more lift during take-offs and landings.
Below: The XF-91 receives the final touches in Farmingdale. The canopy area can be clearly seen to resemble that of the F-84F; also obvious are the four original chambers for the Curtiss-Wright XLR27 rocket engines, two above and two below the exhaust. However, these engines were never installed.

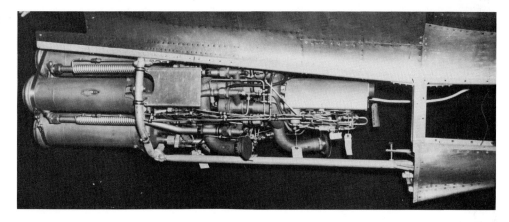

Left: Republic Chief Test Pilot Carl Bellinger, who first flew the XF-91 on 9 May 1949. After surviving numerous test flights in a variety of experimental aircraft, Bellinger was ultimately run over and killed by a drunken driver in 1986. Right: The smaller Reaction Motors XLR11 rocket engines as installed in the Thunderceptor. Now all four chambers are in a diamond pattern below the exhaust.

Below: A front view of the XF-91, showing how the aircraft's unusual, tandem-wheel main landing gear retracted outwards towards the wing tips; the wing roots were too thin to receive the landing gear, which required wheel well doors that hinged near the tips.

allowed the XF-91 to carry external stores, specifically two large fuel tanks each holding 541 US gallons and mounted on a pylon inboard of each main undercarriage unit. The tanks were designed to be dropped when the fighter entered combat.

The tail surfaces of the XF-91 were more conventional, being swept, with some taper on the vertical tail and none on the horizontal stabilizer. The fuselage was considerably fattened at the rear because of the need to incorporate the four rocket motors, and the original design also incorporated a 'butterfly' or vee-type tail assembly intended to create less drag than a conventional tail. Many in the Republic engineering department were concerned about including yet another radical feature in the fighter and thus they overruled the design team, even though wind-tunnel

data were available verifying the practicality of the proposed arrangement. Later, during flight testing, the Air Force insisted on the installation of the 'vee' tail in order to obtain a comparison with the more conventional design that had been used instead, and trials demonstrated that the anticipated drag reduction and subsequent speed increase for the vee-type tail, as well as the predicted improvement in resistance to stall, were well founded. In general, the XF-91's performance was spectacular, with a rate of climb of 40,000ft a minute and a top speed of 984mph.

Flying the XF-91

The Thunderceptor eventually went through a lengthy series of flight tests at Muroc (now Edwards) Air Force Base. On 9 May 1949 Republic's test pilot Carl Bellinger flew the

first prototype on jet power alone for 40 minutes, this first flight proceeding flawlessly and clearly demonstrating the aircraft's excellent qualities. After further trials by Republic, the aircraft was turned over to the Air Force for high-speed and combat-suitability testing. After more months of testing, the afterburner and four rocket motors were installed in order to evaluate the fighter's high-speed characteristics. The rocket motor's highly volatile liquid oxygen (LOX) was stored in two cylindrical tanks in the fuselage over the wing, and to refuel and service the motor Republic was asked by the Air Force to design and build a special refrigerated rig. Weighing 43 tons (and the only truck Republic ever built), it was assembled at Farmingdale and driven across the continent.

On 9 December 1952 the XF-91 was flown beyond Mach 1 through the combined 11,200lb thrust of its jet and rocket engines; this made it the first US combat-type aircraft to exceed the speed of sound in level flight. The transition from subsonic to supersonic flight was made with minimal disturbance. Republic's President, Mundy Peale, then announced optimistically:

The successful conclusion of faster-than-sound flights by the XF-91 means that the nation has bridged the gap between jet planes and rocket planes and this may well be considered in the future as important as was the step from reciprocating engines to jetpower. The things that Republic has learned from the XF-91 will be

incorporated in future production of ultra high-performance aircraft now in various stages of design and development.

However, although the two XF-91s built were intended to be prototypes for similar production fighters, no orders were placed with Republic and the aircraft were subject only to continued testing; jet engine technology advanced meanwhile, to the extent that rocket power was no longer considered indispensable for a high-speed interceptor.

Estimates of the maximum speed that would have been attainable had the Curtiss-Wright XLR27 rocket engine been available for use in the XF-91 were around Mach 2; that using the smaller XLR11 rocket engine was a much less spectacular Mach 1.2. However, the XLR11 never experienced an in-flight failure and on one sortie it proved its value when the XF-91 lost jet power. Unable to restart the J47, the pilot simply fired the rocket motors and was thus able to reach Edwards successfully. In all, it was a relatively trouble-free test programme, the rocket engines performing flawlessly thanks to extensive ground-testing. Later, as radar became a prominent fighter requirement, the first XF-91 was modified with an F-86D type nose with radome and chin inlet.

The XF-91 had a wing span of 31ft 3in, a length of 43ft 3in and a maximum loaded weight of 30,000lb. Its cruising speed was a respectable 539mph, and no armament was ever installed in either aircraft. In many ways

Above: The XF-91 in flight near Edwards AFB, 1950. In spite of the unusual wing configuration, the Thunderceptor proved to be a stable aircraft.

Right: The XF-91 over California, with the third YF-84F in attendance. Note how the dorsal fairing has now been enlarged to hold four XLR11 rocket engines. The Thunderceptor made the first supersonic rocket-powered flight by a US combat aircraft in December 1952; its top speed with rocket power was 984mph.

the XF-91 had a transitional relationship to the F-105, somewhat akin to that between the P-43 the P-47. It really lacked only one crucial ingredient – a powerful engine. But by using data obtained from the design and construction of the XF-91 Kartveli got the powerplant he wanted – an engine 500 per cent more powerful than the J47 – when he designed the F-105, and the idea of a large fighter first proposed in the XF-91 would finally come to fruition.

The XF-103

Even before the XF-91 flew for its first time, the Air Force realized that its short (1,171-mile) range was a major deficiency, the requirement now being for a new, high-speed, area-defence (as opposed to local-defence) interceptor. This led to a new 1950 Air Force Request for Proposals for an 'All-Weather Interceptor' – an aircraft that Republic was also to attempt to develop. The company's offering was to be a huge, triangular-wing design with a

Right: The second XF-91 was eventually modified with a vee-type 'butterfly' tail. The modification worked well and drag was reduced. The bulged lower fairing for the four XLR11 rocket engines is visible here, as is the faired-over upper tailcone. Small, 230-gallon drop tanks are carried.

combination turbojet/ramjet engine and capable of Mach 3 flight – the XF-103.

One of the most advanced aircraft in the history of American aviation – no combat aircraft ever developed would incorporate a greater number of revolutionary features – the XF-103 was also one of the least known. It was to be built of titanium and would also incorporate such innovative features as a pilot escape capsule and a forward-looking periscope. Scores of technical problems had been solved and the construction of the first aircraft was well under way when, in 1957, the Air Force cancelled the programme.

While Republic was developing XF-91 in the late 1940s the company also decided to try to identify the future needs of the Air Force in defending the United States, and to do their best to fulfil them. As a result of these studies, by 1948 Republic was able to design a high-speed aircraft which, it was felt, would satisfy the requirements, and it was this design exercise, combined with Republic's successful XF-91 experience, that ultimately led to the XF-103. Republic's advanced design, designated AP-57, proposed a unique dual-cycle turbo-ramjet engine – a combination of turbojet and ramjet using a common intake and exhaust, i.e., with the turbojet's afterburner section used as a ramjet in order to exceed the main engine's Mach 2 speed limit. Air could be diverted from the main intake around the turbojet and on to the ramjet at the high speeds necessary for the latter to operate, accelerating the aircraft towards Mach 4 (2,600mph).

Republic's original proposal was not acted upon, and following the September 1950 Request for Proposals for a '1954 All-Weather Interceptor' (it was hoped that the aircraft would be operational by 1954), Convair, with its F-102 delta-wing design, was named the winner of the competition. The Air Force nevertheless believed that Republic's advanced project merited further development, taking into consideration both the aircraft's impressive performance estimates and its manufacturer's jet and rocket propulsion experience with the XF-91. Funding was initiated for the expected lengthy development effort which would be required to prove Republic's advanced concept, now officially designated XF-103. By the time of this contract the general design of the XF-103 had been settled.

The design featured a highly streamlined fuselage with a ventral engine intake located approximately at the midpoint. Its length was 81ft and its height 19ft – larger than the future F-105! – and the aircraft's zero-dihedral delta wing was just 36ft in span. The horizontal and vertical tails were also delta-shaped, and towards the end of the programme a folding ventral fin was added to the aft fuselage in order to keep the aircraft directionally stable at speeds above Mach 2.2.

The estimated performance of the XF-103 was remarkable, even by today's standards. The aircraft was to be capable of Mach 3 flight at 60,000ft, with a ceiling of over 75,000ft and a rate of climb of up to 66,000ft a minute! The maximum take-off weight was 43,000lb and the combat radius 430 miles, the limited range being the price to be paid for the aircraft's high speed. However, at the time, the Air Force did not call for long range in its interceptors.

The projected speed of the XF-103 would place the airframe under high aerothermodynamic heating caused by atmospheric friction, and this made the general use of aluminium unacceptable. As a result, the aircraft would be the first to use titanium, with its lightness and strength at high temperatures, as a major structural element. However, in the early 1950s titanium was a relatively unexplored material and it was considered difficult to form, and the XF-103 would thus require major advances in both aerodynamics and materials in order to be successful.

Moreover, in order to fly at the speeds projected, the advanced turbo-ramjet engine needed to be perfected. Curtiss-Wright was called upon to develop the J67-W3 turbojet with an afterburner and ramjet integrated into the propulsion unit. This engine would be a refinement of the Bristol Olympus 'A' of 9,800lb thrust and Curtiss-Wright hoped to be able to uprate it to over 15,000lb on turbojet power alone for 30 minutes, and to 30,000lb at Mach 3 on ramjet power alone. The entire power unit weighed 7,200lb and occupied half the length of the fuselage.

One result of the aircraft's very thin wing section was the necessity to store all the fuel in the fuselage and to supplement the internal fuel with two large external tanks – 3,700 US gallons in total. The horizontal tailplane was to be a one-piece, all-moving stabilator and the ailerons were designed as full-chord, aerodynamically balanced, rotating wing tips.

Above: The Republic XF-103, the most advanced interceptor design of the 1950s, soars over Long Island in this artist's concept. Note the wing-tip ailerons, the protrusion for the periscope, the flush cockpit and the ventral air intake.

The XF-103 also featured flush, streamlined cockpit glazing, eliminating the drag that would be imposed by any protrusions. The original proposals called for an armament of six Hughes GAR-1 Falcon air-to-air guided missiles plus 36 unguided 2.75in Folding-Fin Aircraft Rockets (FFAR). The missiles would be carried in forward bays in the sides of the fuselage and were to be deployed on rails extending into the airstream; the FFARs would also be carried internally, but it was soon realized that unguided rockets would be ineffective for an aircraft of such high speed, so they were eliminated later in the programme.

Design changes

By late 1951 Republic began to realize that progress with the aircraft's engine was lagging and that the J67 would possess inadequate thrust. A later version, the YJ67, was therefore substituted, and the afterburner/ramjet section of the engine was then given its own separate designation, XRJ-55. This engine featured a bypass duct that ran from behind the intake in the lower fuselage, above and parallel to the turbojet and then down into the ramjet section. Flapper-type diverter plates at

each end of the turbojet would be used to redirect incoming air to flow through the bypass duct and into the ramjet, or straight ahead through the turbojet, the transition taking place at a speed of Mach 2 and at an altitude of 50,000ft.

During 1951 a periscope system was selected to improve the pilot's view from the cockpit, but only after several other options were considered, the latter including extensive glazing in the nose (similar to that of the Rainbow), a movable nose section (such as in the later Concorde) and a television camera and screen. Also rejected was a more conventional idea, a standard aircraft canopy with a windscreen shaped much like that of the Douglas Skyrocket. There was even a full-scale mock-up of this proposal, but drag and friction-heating were determined to be too great in this design. The periscope arrangement was selected as it offered the smallest penalty in drag for the forward vision achieved. An F-84G was modified to incorporate the XF-103 periscope system, and this aircraft made a successful cross-country flight in 1955.

Another major system requiring development on the XF-103 was a pilot's escape capsule. Previous experience with pilots ejecting from aircraft moving at high speeds demonstrated the almost certainty of fatal results when ejection occurred above Mach 1 – a problem that Republic recognized early on. Studies indicated that an escape system would of necessity involve the use of a capsule which could be ejected from the aircraft at supersonic speeds and which would protect the pilot during all phases of ejection and descent. The protective capsule also had to be designed to provide stability throughout its trajectory. A variety of designs were explored, including one which involved separating the aircraft's nose section.

The selected design featured a capsule which would contain the aircraft flight controls and be enclosed by a sliding hood and which would be ejected downwards in order to clear the periscope and control panel; all the engine controls and other switches were easily within the pilot's reach when the capsule hood was in the retracted position – as it would be during normal operations. Upon ejection, the hood closed automatically, thus maintaining a pressurized environment. Two booms would extend rearwards at the moment of ejection, with fins to provide stability for the capsule during descent; these fins were curved and formed part of the fuselage skin while the capsule was in place, thereby saving weight. The flight controls in the capsule would automatically connect to linkages in the aircraft when the capsule entered the fuselage. The capsule would ride on rails during catapult ejection, and these same rails would allow the capsule to serve as a lift for

aircraft entry, thereby eliminating the need for ground equipment to enable the aircraft to be boarded. Entry from beneath the cockpit was the most convenient method, but downward ejection removed the possibility of it being activated at zero or low altitude. In total, the capsule weighed 1,100lb and could be ejected successfully at speeds of up to Mach 3.7. A drogue parachute automatically deployed two seconds after ejection, the main 'chute automatically opening when velocity slowed to 260kt and 20,000ft was reached.

In early 1953, prior to Republic's construction of the first XF-103, the Air Force inspected a full-scale mock-up of the aircraft. However, before the construction of a flying prototype began, the Air Force decided to extend the design period of the programme by eighteen months, during which several changes were made (for example, altering the cross-section of the engine exhaust nozzle from square to circular, mainly to save weight). By now the first XF-103 was expected to fly in 1960, following ground tests beginning in 1958, and by 1957 six years and $100 million had been spent on the project. There was as yet no operational aircraft, and Republic proposed utilizing the XF-103's performance by employing the first aircraft as a high-speed, high-altitude research vehicle, aside from its development as an interceptor; the feeling was that not only would this be relevant to the military aspect of the programme, but it would also broaden the base of support for the project in order to ensure its continuation.

In the XF-103's research capacity, Republic proposed placing additional fuel in the

Right: The final design for the XF-103 pilot's escape capsule. Here the hood is in the closed position and the capsule is riding on the elevator rails used for aircraft ingress and egress.

Right: A pilot in a standard 1950s pressure suit sits in the cockpit of the XF-103. The hood is in the open position.

Left: While the XF-103 was being designed a number of different configurations were studied. The more conventional design on the right, similar to that of the Douglas Skyrocket, was rejected in favour of the more streamlined profile on the left. The flush cockpit created far less drag and decreased cooling requirements.
Right: The cockpit in the full-scale mock-up of the XF-103. The wide-vision periscope was sited directly ahead of the pilot, with the radar screen below. The control column can be seen within the hood enclosure.

missile bays and modifying the engine to run on a more powerful fuel: the then promising (but dangerous) 'chemical' fuels, such as heptane, for the ramjet presented the possibility of the XF-103 attaining speeds of Mach 5 – a remarkable prospect given the fact that the fastest aircraft today, 30 years later, can do little better than Mach 2! However, in 1956 the development of the XF-103 stalled when it was learned that the Curtiss-Wright J67 dual-mode powerplant did not perform as expected: it was simply unable to deliver the necessary thrust. In spite of this shortcoming, some elements of the engine were developed and successfully tested in 1956; the transition from turbojet to ramjet, for example, presented no difficulty.

It was believed that one of the main problems in constructing the XF-103 would be in its extensive use of titanium as the primary structural material for the airframe, but in the event assembly was accomplished following conventional construction techniques. One major question was of possible embrittlement in the titanium alloy to be used, and the horizontal stabilizer of the first production XF-103 was manufactured well ahead of schedule in order to serve as a test article. Fortunately no embrittlement was found in the stabilizer, so production could proceed on schedule.

In order to reduce airframe temperatures from skin friction heating, it was also decided to coat the aircraft's surface to increase its ability to radiate heat away from the titanium. This coating, which would reduce skin temperatures from 675 to 600 degrees at Mach 3.7, would have given a blue colour to the XF-103 and was an ancestor of the black coating used on the Lockheed SR-71.

The XF-103's landing gear was simple and sturdy. The main undercarriage was mounted on the fuselage and would retract rearwards under the intake duct. In order to reduce the chances of ingesting foreign objects into the ventral intake the nosewheels swung down below the level of the intake and featured large mudguards for additional protection. The problem of stones kicked up from the runway entering the intake was eliminated by placing a retractable screen ahead of the turbojet.

By mid-August 1957 construction was well advanced on the first XF-103. The fuselage frame was nearly finished and the skin was formed and ready for attachment. The wing framework was also complete and ready for its

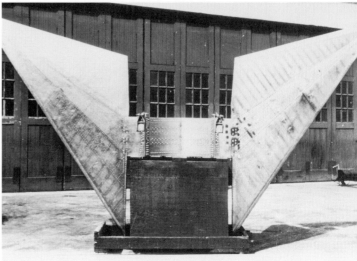

skin sections, while the tail, built earlier, was also ready for attachment. At this point, after so much time and money had been expended on the XF-103 programme, it was cancelled by the Air Force, the August 1957 anouncement citing purely budgetary reasons. However, it was also apparent that the Wright J67 would never provide adequate thrust, and at the time of cancellation Republic was working on the possibility of replacing the J67 with a Bristol Olympus engine of 20,000lb thrust. Today, the estimated performance of the XF-103 is almost equalled only by that of the Lockheed SR-71, although this aircraft can run smoothly and efficiently at supersonic speeds while high-speed flight in the XF-103 would always have pushed the airframe and engine to their limits. The mission foreseen for the XF-103 involved the aircraft loitering some 250 miles north of its base, from which point it was to intercept enemy bombers crossing the Distant Early Warning (DEW) line over Canada, still further to the north.

As soon as the XF-103 programme was cancelled the aircraft under construction was scrapped in order to make room for the production of F-105s. Republic did not have the financial reources necessary to complete the first aircraft for research and demonstration purposes, nor was there reason to do so. Perhaps the greatest lesson to be learned from the fate of the XF-103 is that no matter how promising an aircraft appears to be, if it simply takes too long to develop it will probably be cancelled sooner or later. Had the XF-103 had been finished and flown, the United States would have had an extra-

ordinary Mach 3 fighter in the 1950s. Who knows what impact this would have had upon the subsequent development of fighter aircraft.

The F-105 Thunderchief

By the early 1950s the US Air Force had obtained enough jet experience for it to decide upon an aircraft specifically designed as a fighter-bomber; at about the same time, in 1951, Republic had begun work on an in-house design, Project AP-63 – a single-seat aircraft powered by an Allison J71 and intended to replace the F-84F. It was this AP-63 design that was eventually to evolve into the F-105, the aircraft that carried the major responsibility for the bombing role in the Vietnam War.

The F-105 project began in earnest in October 1952, when the Air Force awarded Republic a contract for pre-production engineering, tooling and material procurement for the development of the aircraft. The engine to be installed in the original YF-105A was to be a Pratt & Whitney J57 engine rather than the proposed J71. The idea for the F-105 was the result of a shift in US strategy after the Korean War towards achieving a global nuclear capability. Accordingly, the Air Force began to stress the F-105's ability to fly long distances carrying a nuclear weapon in a large internal bomb bay. For the next several years this was regarded as the F-105's primary mission; the role in which the F-105 was used in Vietnam – that of a tactical strike aircraft – was a role for which it was never intended.

Above left: A 320-gallon drop tank was later mounted on a more refined version of the XF-103 mock-up.
Above: The completed all-titanium one-piece tail for the XF-103. The first prototype was well advanced when the programme was cancelled.

Right: The first YF-105A at Edwards AFB prior to its maiden flight, 22 October 1955. The basic outline of the F-105 was to remain unchanged until the end of the programme although the YF-105A had a flat-sided fuselage and RF-84F-type wing root intakes. The F-105 is still the largest single-engined, single-seat fighter ever built.

Below: The full-scale mock-up of the XF-103 gives an indication of the aircraft's size and clean lines.

Area rule

The Air Force inspected a mock-up at Republic's premises on 27 October 1953 and a contract for fifteen F-105As was awarded on 28 June 1954. After several changes to the original design, this batch of fifteen aircraft was subdivided into two YF-105As, ten F-105Bs and three photo-reconnaissance RF-105Bs, all with J57 engines. While the first two aircraft were being constructed Republic learned that Convair was experiencing problems with its F-102, encountering transonic drag which could similarly affect the F-105. Thus a new fuselage design for the F-105 was drawn up and the new aircraft was designated F-105B.

Among the most striking of the innovations incorporated into the new jet was the 'coke bottle' shape of its fuselage, designed

Above: A line-up of 1950s products at Farmingdale: (from left to right) an F-105B, an F-84F, an RF-84F and an F-84G.

Left: The F-105 was built to carry a heavy payload, and that it could – several kinds of conventional bombs and rockets, cannon rounds, external fuel tanks and atomic bombs labelled as 'classified'.

according to the NACA 'area rule' principle for reducing air flow drag at transonic speeds. The priniciple dictated that supersonic aircraft be so designed that a cross-section of any portion of the external configuration follow a uniform curve when plotted on a graph, and in the F-105 this was accomplished by 'pinching' the fuselage at the point where the wings were attached and 'swelling out' the other areas.

The aircraft featured swept-forward air intake ducts, located at the wing roots, which inhaled air at tremendous speeds without 'choking' the engine with supersonic shock waves; the ducts' size and shape also contributed to the aircraft's flying stability by shattering shock waves and reducing their effect on the aerodynamically sensitive tail surfaces. A ram-air intake was located at the base of the vertical fin, capturing more air to cool the after end of the aircraft. The F-105's wings had movable wing slats which created a conical camber form along their leading edge, adjustable by the pilot so as to reduce drag at cruising speed and eliminate wing-tip stall at high angles of attack. The F-105 also had a radical 'clover leaf' speed brake that actually formed the last 36in of the fuselage. During braking, these surfaces unfolded like the blossoming petals of a flower to stand out at right angles to the line of flight and serve as a 360-degree air brake which cupped the windstream in perfect balance to slow down the aircraft with great efficiency and stability. A ventral fin was added to the bottom of the rear fuselage to provide greater stability at very high speeds – a legacy of the XF-103 – and the one-piece, flying tailplane (stabilator) gave good longitudinal manoeuvrability at speeds faster

than sound. A drag parachute could also be released by the pilot to slow the jet during landings.

The first YF-105A, now named the Thunderchief, was rolled out of the factory in September 1955, and on 22 October Republic test pilot 'Rusty' Roth conducted the maiden flight of the YF-105A (Air Force serial number 54-098) at Edwards Air Force Base. The aircraft was flown to supersonic speed during the first flight and the transonic drag problem was also confirmed. In December 1955 the second YF-105A was completed.

The Thunderchief was, and still is, the largest single-engine, single-seat aircraft ever built. It was of conventional construction, using 75ST aluminium alloy, steel and titanium. Its standard engine was the Pratt & Whitney J75-19W, delivering a maximum thrust of 26,000lb, and the gross take-off weight was about 50,000lb. It had a relatively small wing span, 35ft, but its length was an amazing 69ft 7in – making it as long as many Second World War bombers. Its maximum speed was Mach 1.2 at sea level, and Mach 2.1 at 50,000ft. The F-105 carried no fuel in its wing, it being accommodated in the fuselage and in external fuel tanks (most of the inner wing was taken up by the large wheel wells). Tactical range with a full bomb load was about 300 miles, although this could be extended by aerial refuelling; over Vietnam, Thunderchiefs normally rendezvoused with KC-135 tankers soon after take-off and again after leaving the combat zone.

On a mission over North Vietnam the F-105 normally carried six 750lb bombs or five 1,000-pounders, along with two 450 US gallon drop tanks; the bomb bay, which was as large as

Left: An in-flight
demonstration of
Republic's 'buddy'
refuelling system
involving a YF-105A
(above) and an F-105B.
Note the taller vertical
tail of the F-105B.

that of a B-17 and could carry 50 per cent more ordnance, could also accept an auxiliary 390 US gallon fuel tank. The armament could also include Sidewinder air-to-air missiles, AGM-12 Bullpup air-to-surface missiles and a 20mm General Electric M-61 Vulcan rotary cannon which fired at a rate of 6,000 rounds a minute and was extremely effective in strafing ground targets as well as engaging enemy aircraft.

In April 1956 Republic received the go-ahead to build five F-105C two-seaters, with a very large, single canopy over both cockpits, designed to Training Command specifications. However, the contract was terminated in October 1957 and the F-105C was never built. April 1956 also saw the completion of the first F-105B, Republic's test pilot 'Hank' Beaird undertaking the maiden flight. This aircraft, equipped with a J75P-3 engine, reached a top of 1,420mph (Mach 2.15) during trials. In July that year the RF-105B was cancelled, but the three original RF-105s were to be completed

as JF-105Bs and used as flight-test vehicles without photographic equipment. These three machines, the first of which flew on 18 July 1957, served as flying test-beds for the flutter test programme, the autopilot development programme, the external stores performance and jettison programmes and many other development trials through the years 1957–61. The first F-105B to be delivered to an Air Force tactical unit went to the 335th Squadron of the 4th Tactical Wing in May 1958. This squadron, commanded by Col. Robert Scott, was deployed to Eglin Air Force Base to perform service testing of the F-105B weapon system. By January 1959 the F-105B was declared operational, 63 examples serving with the 4th Fighter Wing. In June 1959 the 4th Tactical Fighter Wing completed its first year of flying the F-105B without major incident, and the Thunderchief thus became the first aircraft in service history to have achieved such a safety record. The F-105B also performed one

Below: An early F-105B photographed at Republic's factory. The aircraft now had a 'coke bottle' fuselage and forward-swept wing-root intakes.
Below right: The third F-105B, by now named the Thunderchief. The pilot required a long ladder to enter the massive aircraft.

Above left: Despite the aircraft's size, nine F-105Bs were modified for use by 'The Thunderbirds' for the 1964 season although, as it happened, the Thunderchiefs performed at only a few shows.

Left: The JF-105B was to be the prototype for the reconnaissance version of the F-105; note the flat-sided nose section for oblique camera positions. The RF-105 was never developed, however, and the JF-105B was employed by Republic for various trials.

Above: Upon landing, F-105s deployed a parachute to shorten the landing roll. Here a JF-105B touches down at Republic. Note that the flaps are fully deployed and the split 'petal' speed brakes open.

Right: F-105Bs roll off Republic's assembly line in Building 17.

unusual feat. On 11 December 1959 Brig. Gen. Joseph Moore, Commander of the 4th TFW, set a new world speed record of 1,216.4mph for the 100km closed course at Edwards AFB in Operation 'Fastwind'. Remarkably, F-105Bs also served with the US Air Force's aero-batic team 'The Thunderbirds' during part of the 1965 season.

All-weather capability

Only 75 F-105Bs were built, for soon after production began the Air Force suggested to Republic that advances in electronics might make it possible to give the Thunderchief an all-weather ground-attack capability. In response, Republic developed the F-105D, incorporating its 'Thunderstick' system, which was at the time the most sophisticated all-weather navigation and weaponry delivery package to be installed in a single-seat aircraft. In October 1957 twenty F-105Ds were ordered together with eight F-105Es. The all-weather F-105D had integrated electronic and

Top left: The F-105's four brakes could be opened in flight or on the ground to reduce the aircraft's speed quickly.
Above: The training version of the Thunderchief, the F-105C, never got beyond mock-up form in 1956. The two-man crew would have been carried under one large canopy.
Left: F-105Bs nearing final assembly at Farmingdale.

radar systems giving it blind weapon-delivery capability; the E model was to have been a two-seat, all-weather fighter-bomber but financial considerations caused this order to be rescinded in 1959 and be replaced by the procurement of an additional quantity of Ds. The first F-105D was flown at Farmingdale on 9 June 1959, one month ahead of schedule, and ultimately some 610 of the type were produced, making them the major variant of the Thunderchief.

The F-105D's advanced electronics included its ASG-19 fire control, an integrated armament control system consisting of radar, an automatic lead-computing sight, a toss-bomb computer and associated equipment. It had APN-131 all-weather doppler navigation and the all-purpose NASARR monopulse radar which was able to attack targets through fog and darkness, NASARR providing all radar functions for both low-level and high-level missions – air search, automatic tracking, ground mapping, terrain avoidance and target display. Its fully integrated General Electric FC-5 navigational, fire control and flight control system made it possible for a pilot to take off in foul, zero-ceiling weather, fly 'blind' to the target, come in low 'on the deck' beneath radar detection, and unleash his ordnance.

The year 1960 saw the F-105D's introduction to the Air Force inventory, the 335th TFS

replacing its older models with the newer all-weather version. The Thunderchief's first European deployment came in May 1961 when the 36th TFW at Bitburg, Germany, received its first F-105Ds.

By early 1961 new emphasis was being placed on conventional weapons by Department of Defense planners, and in June that year the F-105 impressively demonstrated its ability to meet the challenge by dropping the heaviest load of bombs ever carried by a single-engined fighter – seven tons of bombs, released during special tests at Eglin Air Force Base, Florida; in October 1961 two F-105s from the 4th TFW repeated this performance at Fort Bragg, North Carolina, with President Kennedy as one of the witnesses. As a result of these demonstrations, and at the direction of the Air Force, this additional capability for conventional weapon

Above: One of the earliest F-105Ds sits on the ramp at Eglin AFB during weapons testing; a Bullpup missile hangs from the port wing. The F-105D was a vastly improved model incorporating a more powerful engine, a redesigned cockpit, an all-weather navigation and fire-control system and the ability to refuel in flight using either the flying boom or the probe and drogue system.

Left: The nose of the F-105 contained a variety of access panels. Of special note is the emergency wind-driven hydraulic generator on the lower fuselage, a device which proved especially valuable to damaged aircraft in Vietnam.

Above: A Tactical Air Command F-105D over the California Desert. The huge 450-gallon drop tanks had a slight nose-down attitude on the ground but were aligned with the in-flight attitude to reduce drag. This photograph encapsulates the power, yet grace, of the 1,400mph F-105.

Right: Twenty F-105D nose sections under construction in 1962 reveal the scale of Republic's assembly line. The inactivity has been caused by an employees' strike.

carriage was ordered for new production aircraft and planned as a retrofit on earlier versions of the F-105. Of the 610 F-105Ds that were built, thirty were modified with the 'T-Stick II' bombing system and featured a deep dorsal fairing from the cockpit to the fin.

In August 1962 Republic received the go-ahead to build the F-105F, another two-seat variant, similar to the cancelled F-105E in that it was intended as a pilot trainer for the complex weapon system. However, the F-105F in fact became a combat aircraft in Vietnam, its second seat occupied by the Electronic Countermeasures Operator, and was to reign supreme as a surface-to-air missile (SAM) suppressor. The first F-105F was flown 40 days ahead of schedule, on 11 June 1963. Of the 143 F-105Fs that were built, the last 48 were modified into F-105Gs and were fitted with fuselage pods containing jamming equipment and new combat/event recorders.

The F-105 in Vietnam
When the US Air Force found itself committed in Vietnam it was ill-equipped to fight a conventional war and the F-105 was therefore pressed into service as a pure bomber. The subsequent performance of the Thunderchief over North Vietnam was all the more remarkable because the aircraft was clearly not designed for the role it was now about to play: the F-105D was designed as a carrier of

Left: Ordnancemen load
20mm rounds into an
F-105's rotary cannon.
This weapon was used to
great effect in Vietnam.
Below left: Brand new
F-105Ds sit on the ramp
outside Republic's
factory.
Right top: An F-105D
fires all 38 unguided
FFARs from its two
rocket pods during a
tactical training mission.
Right, centre: In 1961, at
Fort Bragg in North
Carolina, this F-105D
took off on a
demonstration flight with
six tons of bombs to set
a new world weight-
lifting record for a single-
engined aircraft.
Right, bottom: The
F-105D's cockpit, unlike
that of earlier models,
incorporated radar and
strip gauges.

Left: An F-105D of the 44th TFS receives fuel from a KC-135 over Vietnam; F-105s were normally refuelled both inbound and outbound from the target. The Thunderchief was one of the first USAF aircraft in Vietnam to be camouflaged following the General Order in 1966.

nuclear weapons, conventional ordnance being almost an afterthought. To retrofit the F-105 for the conventional role, special bomb racks had to be rigged under the wings and fuselage. However, such external carriage increased the aircraft's drag and reduced its speed and manoeuvrability, and on flights over the North the F-105s would have to face MiGs, surface-to-air missiles, intense flak and even automatic-weapon fire. Perhaps surprisingly, the F-105 managed to bring down 29 MiGs in combat, and without missiles and bombs hung all over it, and at low altitudes, the Thunderchief could take on and defeat the then-modern MiG-21. Surface-to-air missiles and flak proved more difficult to evade, however, and Thunderchief pilots in Vietnam encountered the densest flak concentrations

ever experienced by American pilots. The defences surrounding cities in Germany and Japan during the Second World War did not compare to the number of guns and missiles ringing Hanoi and Haiphong.

The first F-105 squadrons for the Vietnam War were formed in 1965 – the 335th TFW at Takhili and the 388th at Korat, Thailand. The first Thunderchief raid took place in March 1965, on the Xom Bang ammunition storage facility, and most of the early attacks were aimed at targets just north of the Demilitarized Zone (DMZ). In 1966 and 1967 Operation 'Rolling Thunder' strikes were begun. Intended to destroy the ability of North Vietnam to wage war, these attacks were, in the main, aimed at bridges and industrial targets. North Vietnam was

Left: Early in the Vietnam War F-105s were used as bombers to destroy tactical targets, such as the Xon Phoung highway and railroad bridges in August 1966. However, because of their high attrition rate, the aircraft were subsequently employed against enemy missile sites.

Right: An F-105D cartridge start was a noisy, smoky affair. In this photograph taken at Takhli, Thailand, during the Vietnam War, a full load of bombs is just visible through the smoke.

Right: An F-105D of the 355th TFW, based at Takhli, Thailand, during the Vietnam War, has its J75 engine changed in a hot revetment. The positioning trailer is obviously heavy and difficult to move.

Right: F-105Ds in Vietnam carried a variety of ordnance. Early on, the Bullpup air-to-ground missile was a popular weapon. Each F-105 could carry two, as well as two external tanks and a third inside the bomb bay.

defended by 8,000 anti-aircraft guns and 300 SAM sites, plus MiGs and ground fire, and, needless to say, F-105 losses mounted as the missions got more hazardous. In the bombing role, Thunderchiefs would follow a mountain ridge ('Thud Ridge') from the north-west towards targets in the Hanoi area.

Perhaps the most famous F-105 raid occurred on 2 August 1967. The Doumer Bridge north of Hanoi, vital for moving war supplies by rail between China and North Vietnam, had been removed from the list of restricted targets and the 335th and 388th were determined to destroy it. Maintenance men had already loaded the F-105s for a lesser target when they learned – at the last moment – that they had to download that ordnance in order to substitute 3,000lb bombs for use against the bridge. The pilots were quickly briefed and, led by former X-15 test pilot Col. Robert White and flying against one of the most heavily defended targets of the war, the Thunderchiefs succeeded in knocking the structure out. Fourteen SAMs were fired at the raiders but not one aircraft was shot down. The bridge was eventually repaired, but it was hit and knocked out again – several times.

By 1969 F-105Ds were generally confined to bombing targets in Laos (where there was less anti-aircraft fire) and by 1970 they had been withdrawn from Vietnam altogether. However, during the course of the war, F-105s had accounted for more than 75 per cent of all Air Force missions flown over North Vietnam.

Wild Weasel

Throughout the war the North Vietnamese made extensive use of Soviet radar-guided SAM-2s, which exacted unacceptable US losses, and to counter these the two-seat F-105F – the most successful of the Thunderchief versions – was called into action. Most F models were fitted with electronic counter-measures (ECM) equipment and were called 'Wild Weasels', their task to jam the search radar of SAM positions and then destroy them with their Shrike missiles. The F-105F would wait for a SAM site to come 'on the air' (launch a missile) and they then quickly fired their radar-guided Shrike missiles into the launch site. A Wild Weasel normally accompanied each flight of two or four F-105Ds – a technique which helped to cut the loss rate of the latter.

Far left: In spite of its size the F-105 was also a 'MiG killer' over Vietnam. This MiG-17 was one of 29 F-105 victims.
Left: Lt David Waldrop shot down two MiG-17s on 23 August 1967 in his F-105D.
Right: Although not designed as a tactical bomber, the F-105 could take severe punishment and keep flying. This F-105 received a large hole in its starboard wing from anti-aircraft fire yet it returned safely to base.
Below: Anti-aircraft fire could blow off the top of a fin but it could not stop this Thunderchief.

Left: Flying from Korat with the 388th TFW, this F-105D took a direct hit from a Soviet 'Atoll' air-to-air missile and still made it back to base. Above: The first F-105F at Farmingdale, June 1963. The F model was intended as a two-seat, all-weather aircraft for training as well as combat missions but most saw service in Vietnam as Wild Weasel SAM-site destroyers and flak-suppression aircraft. Right: A late production F-105F of the 562nd TFS. The F had a longer fuselage and a larger vertical tail. The second cockpit was used for the Electronic Warfare Officer. The mission of the F-105F in Vietnam was simple: Wild Weasel crews were to protect the strike force by suppressing enemy air defence systems, a task normally accomplished through the use of radar-seeking Shrike missiles and cannon fire.

The first F-105Fs were introduced into Vietnam in 1966 as replacements for F-100 Wild Weasels, and the F and G models remained in South-East Asia until the end of US involvement, eventually being employed 'riding shotgun' for the high-flying B-52s. The F-105's last major action began in April 1972 when the North Vietnamese invaded the South. The Wild Weasels then went into the North with the B-52s during the 'Linebacker I' and 'Linebacker II' operations, destroying enemy missile sites, until December 1972 when North Vietnam was at last forced to come to the bargaining table.

The accomplishments of the Thunderchief in combat are almost legendary but the air crews paid a heavy price: of the 833 F-105s produced between 1958 and 1964, 382 were shot down over Vietnam, and in 1967 alone 200 were lost to enemy fire. These losses seem excessive, but in fact the average mission loss rate during the early phase of the war was only one per cent – which gives an indication of how hard the aircraft were worked.

In spite of the aircraft's faults – for example, it could not turn as well as most other fighters and the hydraulic lines were located too close together – most pilots who flew the F-105 liked it. It could go faster and further, with more bombs, than any fighter in the world; it was an extremely accurate platform for weapons deliveries; and it could take a lot of damage

and keep flying. The men who appreciated the F-105 most were those who took direct hits over Hanoi or Haiphong and flew back to Thailand with part of their wing missing, a stabilizer shot off or zero oil pressure. MiGs also took a high toll of F-105s. Thunderchiefs were often attacked while still fully loaded with bombs inbound to a target, but even so the F-105 pilots would often try to use their high speed to keep the MiGs at bay rather than jettison their bombs. Once the latter were dropped, however, an F-105 could easily outrun a MiG.

In all, Thunderchiefs flew 101,000 strike mission in Vietnam. In doing so they hit 12,675 targets and dropped 202,596 tons of bombs. The last F-105s to fly were the Fs of the 419th TFW at Hill Air Force Base, Utah, which were phased out on 25 February 1984. Republic had expected Thunderchief production to continue beyond 1964 but US Secretary of Defense Robert McNamara terminated the project, opting instead for the development of a fighter-bomber (to become the much troubled TFX or F-111) that both the Air Force and Navy could use.

Upon completion of the F-105 programme, Alexander Kartveli retired as full-time head of Republic's design department. However, he remained with the company as a consultant, assisting in the devlopment of several new aircraft projects through to the 1960s and early 1970s.

Left: Heading North. This one photograph summarizes Thunderchief operations in Vietnam. An F-105D, nearer the camera, carries Bullpup missiles to destroy a ground target; prior to his run, the F-105F (background) will try to knock out any SAM sites around the target with his Shrike missiles. F-105s in Vietnam normally flew in teams of two or four, evenly divided with D and F models.
Above right: In 1966 thirty F-105Ds were modified with the much improved 'T'-Stick II' all-weather bombing system. These aircraft could be distinguished by their large dorsal spines that covered the new electronics systems.
Right: The last version of the Thunderchief was the two-seat F-105G; this is one from the 57th FWW. Over 120 Fs were converted to Gs, principally by incorporating greatly improved avionics for the Wild Weasel mission. Additional electronic countermeasures equipment was housed in blisters on the sides of the fuselage (visible just below the wing).

Spaceflight and Other Ventures

REPUBLIC'S INVOLVEMENT in the field of missiles began towards the end of the Second World War, when company engineers received a quantity of German V1 fragments which they pieced together. The German V1 'Buzz Bomb' was actually a pilotless flying bomb that flew a pre-set course at the comparatively low speed of 400mph, this weakness making it vulnerable to fighter attack and anti-aircraft fire and accounting for the fact that over half of the 8,000 launched were destroyed in flight. However, those that struck their targets killed nearly 6,000 people and destroyed or damaged 75,000 homes. First launched against London in June 1944,

the V1 was the world's first operational long-range missile.

Realizing the potential of the weapon, the US Army formulated plans for producing duplicates. Several wrecked specimens were flown specially from Great Britain to the United States, the first parts arriving as early as 9 July 1944 at Wright Field. Seventeen days later the Ford Motor Company had built a complete copy of the Argus pulse jet engine incorporating original and copied parts.

The JB-2

A manufacturer to produce airframes was required, and in October 1944 the Republic

Above: JB-2s began to roll off Republic's assembly lines just two months after the company received a captured German V1. The US Army and Navy planned to launch them from ships during the expected invasion of Japan but the end of the war precluded this. Republic oversaw the production and testing of some 1,200 examples; this particular JB-2 was used on a War Bond tour.

Left: The Republic JB-2 under construction early in 1945. Essentially US copies of the German V1 'Buzz Bomb', the JB-2s, built at Farmingdale, provided the earliest American experience in land-based missile production and operation.

Aviation Corporation was contracted to produce duplicates of the V1, to be designated JB-2 and different only in minor detail and in a more simplified and accurate system of flight controls; one fairly complete V1 was apparently sent to Republic, and this was reworked as the prototype JB-2. Once production began, the Republic airframes were mated with Ford pulse-jet engines and sent to Wright Field for wind-tunnel testing, and by November the existence of these missiles was being announced as an accomplished fact by the news media. Republic's first JB-2s were delivered in January, just three months later, and after successful tests at Wright Field further JB-2 production was sent directly to Eglin Field in north-western Florida for operational trials. The JB-2s used pulse-jet engines essentially identical to the German originals, in which air was admitted in pulses, unlike a turbojet which requires a continuous flow. However, in order for the pulse jet to function, its vehicle had first to achieve flying speed: the engine could not propel the missile from a standstill. A gyrocompass, set before launch, would guide the missile towards its target, and after a pre-determined period a timing device would cut off the engine and the missile would dive to the ground.

At Eglin, Army engineers built two long, concrete take-off ramps, one inclined at 6 degrees and the other horizontal; explosion-proof shelters, watch-towers and barracks were also built. However, the American missiles were launched in somewhat different fashion from their German counterparts: the V1 was fired from its ramp by a large moving piston whereas the JB-2 was launched by means of four 4,000lb thrust solid-fuel rocket boosters. After some fifty firings, the Army felt that it had a dependable missile with a range of 150 miles and a maximum speed of 440mph. Both the US Army and Navy seriously considered firing JB-2s into Japan prior to the expected invasion, but the dropping of the atomic bomb and subsequent end of the war prevented the missile's operational use. However, trials continued in the postwar period. The US Navy launched several JB-2s (named 'Loons') from specially modified submarines and ships. These were the first missiles ever fired from US Navy vessels and the last launchings took place in 1950.

The Republic JB-2 was 27ft long and had an 18ft wing span; its empty weight was 1,965lb and it could carry a 2,080lb warhead in the nose. Construction was almost entirely of steel. After manufacturing the first several dozen examples, Republic subcontracted further production though remained in the programme in a supervisory capacity. Altogether some 1,200 JB-2s were built, and they provided the Americans with their first experience in the production and operation of guided missiles.

In 1952, wanting to draw on their valuable experience with the JB-2, and realizing that the development of new missiles could be highly lucrative in the dawning jet age, Republic established a separate Guided Missiles Division. Progress in the research and

development of these advanced weapons was rapid, and in 1954 the Division was relocated at a new plant in Hicksville, Long Island, to accommodate guided missiles engineering and research departments, electronics and servo-mechanisms laboratories and a missiles prototype assembly shop.

Drones

Although much of the Missile Division's work was secret, the US Army revealed in August 1957 that Republic had been awarded contracts for the development and production of two combat surveillance systems for the Signal Corps, one a propeller-driven reconnaissance drone and the other an advanced jet drone. Both were to be operated by Army units in the battle area, in any weather, using photographic, radar and infra-red techniques, and both were to be zero-launched and recoverable by the unit operating them.

Republic's first production drone was the SD-3 of 1957–58. Won after an industry-wide competition, it was for short-range surveillance and was driven by a conventional engine and pusher propeller; its purpose was to report on enemy gun emplacements, troop

Above: The Republic SD-3 combat surveillance drone of 1958. The SD-3 was a short-range system driven by a conventional engine and propeller. One of the first such American drones, it could use photography, radar, TV or infra-red sensory devices simply by having its nose units changed.

Left: Republic's SD-4 Swallow of 1960 was a jet-powered surveillance drone, again developed for the US Army. Produced by the company's new Missile Systems Division (as was the SD-3), it was launched by solid-fuel booster rockets and recovered by parachute and used radar, infra-red or photography for its mission.

movements and tank concentrations. Republic's $1.7 million contract called for a rapid schedule of detailed design and the immediate fabrication of initial service test units for the Army, and the first SD-3 was rolled out on 18 August 1958. Flight testing, begun on 20 January 1959, was conducted at the Army Test Center at Yuma in Arizona. After launch the drone would be directed through a series of test manoeuvres, and a recovery sequence, involving the deployment of parachute and landing bags, was then initiated.

The SD-3 was one of the first combat survillance drones developed for the US Army. It had an air-to-ground 'spy' system, one of the most advanced sensor devices developed up to this time, and could be switched over from photography to radar, TV or infra-red sensory devices simply by interchanging the nose units. It was 15ft 3in long and 11ft 2in wide and cruised at 300mph at 20,000ft; power was supplied by a Continental 10-200 engine and twin JATO

rockets gave the drone a zero-launching capability. However, although 50 were built for test purposes, the SD-3 was not placed into operational service.

The jet-powered, delta-winged Republic SD-4 Swallow was built in 1960–61 under a $3 million contract for the study, development, design and production of test models. A medium-range, combat surveillance drone designed to provide targeting information of high accuracy, it was zero-launched, recoverable and contained advanced observation equipment such as photographic, radar and infra-red devices in interchangeable nose units which could be fitted quickly in the field. Designed for all-weather operations, the SD-4 had a length of 30ft 5in and a wing span of 11ft 6in and was powered by a Pratt & Whitney JT-12 turbojet. It cruised at Mach 1.5 at 40,000ft and had a range of 300 miles.

From 1960 the Missile Systems Division of Republic conducted a feasibility study to provide the design criteria for a lightweight,

Below: In 1965 Republic developed the simple, low-cost Bikini Aerial Drone Reconnaissance System – essentially a large model aircraft with a camera. The drone was to weigh no more than 50lb for ease of movement and operation by two men.

Antenna

Lights

PRC10

Frequency Test Set
(used for PRC10 only)

low-cost, fair-weather photographic aerial reconnaissance system for use by Marine Battalion landing teams, and this resulted in a 1965 contract to develop the Bikini Aerial Drone Reconnaissance System for battlefield surveillance by combat units. The system consisted of a small, radio-controlled drone and supporting ground equipment. The drone was a conventional, high-wing, propeller-driven aircraft that was catapulted to flying speed in a distance of 6ft by a pneumatic launcher and was recovered by parachute. In addition to the launcher, the ground equipment included a manual engine starter, a radio transmitter, a drone control box and a compact film processor-viewer and enlarger-printer; an entire system, including two drones, fitted into a standard jeep-drawn trailer. Operated by a two-man team, the Bikini system could provide finished 9 × 9 aerial photographs within 30 minutes of arrival at an unprepared

site. Equipped with a 4.5hp two-stroke engine, the Bikini was built of fibreglass and light-weight aluminium and the aircraft had a length of 6ft and a wing span of 7ft.

The Bikini was required to weigh no more than 50lb, for ease of movement and operation, and be operable by a crew with minimal training (in actuality it was found that personnel without prior experience in manned or model aircraft could successfully pilot the Bikini after one hour's training). In July and August 1966 operational tests were conducted by the First Drone Platoon of the Second Marine Division at Camp Lejune, North Carolina. Expert riflemen participating in these tests fired 1,300 rounds, striking the flying drone only seven times. The Bikini was originally developed by Republic under the sponsorship of the Office of Naval Research on behalf of the Marine Corps. The original contract called for Republic to deliver 25

Below: The Bikini system was designed to be transportable by a standard Army jeep and trailer and its 'pilots' required but one hour's training. The drone was tracked by radar and recovered by parachute. Originally intended for Marine Corps use, it first saw service in 1966.

drones and five ground support units to the Corps, and this was followed by a further order for 36 militarized units. The entire programme was completed in two years.

The Bikini had a range of ten miles and could fly at 80mph for thirty minutes. Its service ceiling was 10,000ft, although most photographs were take at 1,000ft. Setting up consisted of attaching the wings and tail, fuelling, and installing the film and could be accomplished in 15min. The heart of the system was a Fairchild 70mm camera which could take up to 80 photographs once the starting impulse was given. The drone was radar-tracked, so the controller could order it to take photographs, once over the desired target, by pressing a button on the control stick. When the mission was over the operator flew the drone back to the recovery area and pressed the parachute release button. After the drone returned from its mission the film

was placed immediately in a portable processor, where it was conjoined with a roll of saturated processing web; finished film was available for viewing minutes later, and the drone could be refuelled, have its parachute repacked and be ready for flight in 15min. The Bikini system was briefly deployed in Vietnam during 1967.

Diversification

In an attempt to diversify from fixed-wing aircraft, Republic formed a Helicopter Division in late 1957 to handle the sales, service and production of the French Alouette and Djinn helicopters. Under a licencing agreement with Sud Aviation of France, the Alouette and Djinn would be assembled, flight-tested, marketed and serviced by Republic, the initial manufacture of all components and engine taking place in France; the fabrication of the entire aircraft

Below: The Republic Bikini system had a range of ten miles at 80mph. Most of its photographs were taken at 1,500ft – such as this one showing Republic's Farmingdale Field. Up to eighty photographs could be taken on each mission.

Left: In an attempt to diversify, Republic formed a Helicopter Division to handle the sales, service and production of French Alouette and Djinn helicopters. In 1958 the Alouette became the first French aircraft to be granted American certification. Republic closed the Division when sales did not live up to expectations.

Below left: In 1963 Republic signed an agreement with Vickers Ltd of Great Britain to manufacture and market the VA-3 hovercraft. The 12-ton VA-3 could travel at 65mph over land or sea, hovering on a cushion of air. Two turbine engines provided lift, two others gave forward propulsion. The VA-3 could carry 24 passengers but no US orders were forthcoming and Republic halted the programme.

would eventually have been carried out by Republic. On 14 January 1958 the Alouette was granted a Certificate of Airworthiness by the CAA; it was the first French aircraft of any kind, and the first turbine-powered helicopter in the world, to received American certification. In all, Republic sold about sixty commercial Alouettes in the United States and Canada. The helicopter carried five people at a top speed of 110mph. It was 31ft long and 6ft 10in wide and was driven by a Turboméca Artouste II turbine engine. In addition to rescue and passenger-carrying duties, the Alouettes were used as aerial cranes and for crop-dusting and patrolling.

In September 1958 the Sud Djinn was demonstrated to Republic. The Djinn (French for Little Devil) was a small, two-seat helicopter powered by a unique jet engine system. Republic was licenced to assemble and sell the helicopter and the company, appreciating the aircraft's extreme manoeuvrability, hoped for sales to the US military as an anti-tank vehicle. Jet power gave the Djinn an extreme rate of climb, 6000ft a minute, and allowed it to operate in extremes of temperature and altitude. The jet thrust was routed through the tips of the rotor, and thus no torque was produced and the need for a tail rotor was obviated. The Djinn was 17ft 5in long and 6ft 4in wide and was powered by a Turboméca Palouste IV engine. No sales were forthcoming however, and by 1961 Republic closed its helicopter division.

In the early 1960s Republic began to branch out of aerospace entirely, establishing new programmes for the manufacture of various types of ships and experimental automobiles. In 1963 the company signed a contract with Vickers Ltd and Hovercraft Development of Great Britain for the development, manufacture and marketing of the VA-3 hovercraft. The VA-3, which had gone into commercial service in Britain in 1962, was a revolutionary GEM (Ground Effect Machine) which had no contact with the surface when it was operating; it floated on a cushion of air and was thus able to operate over land, water, marsh, snow and ice with equal impunity. It was a twelve-ton, four-engined vehicle able to carry 24 passengers. Republic purchased one VA-3 which was berthed at the company's Montauk, Long Island, ocean-front facility. It was used to investigate the applications of the hovercraft principle to a wide range of operating conditions, including military use. However, apart from one US Marine Corps study contract, no orders for the vehicle were forthcoming and Republic ceased development along this line in 1964.

Republic also briefly delved into other nautical ventures, including a proposed naval hydrofoil gunboat named the 'Thunderaider' in 1963. It also participated in the construction of an experimental Navy submarine, the X-1, and attempted to manufacture small aluminium 'swamp boats'. The company did receive one construction contract from the US

Below: In 1964 Republic built its only submarine, the experimental X-1 for the US Navy. It was 49ft long, weighed 30 tons and could carry a four- or five-man crew.

Left: In 1964 Republic also investigated the small-boat market and designed its flat-bottomed 'swamp boat'. However Republic's efforts at diversification consistently failed – the aluminium boat market was already dominated by neighbouring Grumman.

Navy in 1962, for designing and building a submarine trainer for officers and crews of atomic Polaris-type and attack submarines. This trainer went into operation at the Navy's Fleet Ballistic Missile Training Facility at Charleston, South Carolina, in 1963. However, by 1965 all nautical ventures at Republic were terminated since they had met with little success.

Republic's ventures took on an entirely new complexion in 1965 when the company was awarded a contract to design an experimental 'Safety Car' for New York State. The automobile was unique in that its principal design objectives were accident avoidance and injury reduction. Indeed, criteria were developed and analyses preformed in five categories of automobile safety: accident avoidance, crash

Left: The Republic Submarine Trainer, in 1962. Built under a US Navy contract, it was used to train officers and crews for atomic Polaris-type and attack submarines.

Right: The Republic 'Safety Car', designed under a New York State contract in 1965. Its primary mission was accident avoidance and injury reduction, but New York cancelled the contract after the design stage. The car's aerodynamic styling is evident.

injury reduction, pedestrian injury reduction, post-crash protection and non-operating safety. These critical elements were examined to determine the scope and character of existing problems, and to define the major influencing factors and relationships that would be incorporated into the Car, the primary objective of the systems engineering approach to these problems being to produce a properly functioning integrated system that would meet the needs of vehicle safety in the most efficient manner. Republic had hoped to construct twelve to fifteen of the experimental vehicles at a cost of several million dollars, but New York State decided not to proceed with the project after the design stage.

Nevertheless, in 1966 Republic won a follow-up contract to design and build a new safety car for the Federal Department of Transportation, and excitement was high as this seemed to be the company's first successful non-aerospace venture. The contract was to design, explore and construct a vehicle with safety capabilities which would make possible the legislative establishment of safety definitions and standards applicable to all vehicles. The Experimental Safety Vehicle built by Republic, a streamlined vehicle with clean lines derived from the company's aerospace background, had four doors and accommodated a driver and four passengers. It was about the size of a conventional four-

Right: The 1966 Fairchild-Republic Safety Car, as produced at Farmingdale for the Federal Department of Transportation. Republic designed and built a vehicle with capabilities which would make possible the legislative establishment of safety definitions and standards applicable to all vehicles. The vehicle could withstand crashes at 50mph. Note the extended bumper and rooftop periscope. Although a short-lived programme, Republic's Safety Car had an influence which is still being felt today.

door American saloon and could withstand front- and rear-end barrier crashes at 50mph and side collisions at 40mph; a wrap-around bumper protected the vehicle from low-speed damage at all angles. There was a blunt, energy-absorbing front end that afforded maximum protection to pedestrians, and the foam-filled bumpers automatically extended 12in at speeds exceeding 30mph. An over-the-roof periscope provided wide-angle rear vision, while visibility was further enhanced by the large window areas on the car. The vehicle's fully unitized body structure was representative of the stressed, reinforced skin techniques derived from aerospace concepts.

Ultimately the Department of Transportation directed Republic to build two of the cars, which were enthusiastically received and underwent a successful testing programme. Apparently the company had hoped to profit from patent rights from the project, but this never transpired and Republic lost money on the venture. However, the influence of the Republic Safety Car is still felt in America to this day: by the mid-1980s most US cars had a third brake light in the rear window, as well as rounded bumper ends and flush door handles for added pedestrian safety – all features pioneered by the Republic Safety Car.

Top: In order to supplement meagre aircraft sales in the 1960s, Republic secured various subcontracts. Between 1962 and 1974, for example, the company produced over 4,000 tail sections for the McDonnell F-4 Phantom fighter.

Above: One very successful Republic subcontract involved the building of wing control surfaces for the Boeing 747. Here one of over 600 sets of 747 ailerons heads for the West Coast.

Subcontracts

In order to make up for meagre aircraft sales in the 1960s, Republic supplemented production with various subcontracts. Beginning in 1962, the company became a major subcontractor to McDonnell Douglas for the fabrication of F-4 Phantom aft fuselage sections, including fin, stabilator and engine access doors: between 1962 and 1974 over 4,000 such units were built under a $354 million contract. The F-4 aft section weighed 2,000lb, 1,000 of which were titanium and most of the remainder mag-nesium, steel and aluminium. By the late 1960s Republic had won a $35 million contract to design and build the aft fuselage and vertical fin for the US (Boeing) Supersonic Transport. In fact, the company invested $3 million in the SST program and even erected a new building for production, but the programme was terminated by Congress in 1971.

In 1966 Republic was selected to engineer and produce the wing control surfaces of the Boeing 747 'Jumbo Jet', taking responsibility for the design and fabrication of all leading-edge flaps, spoilers, ailerons and trailing-edge flaps. The total weight of the wing control surfaces was 9,250lb. Under this $228 million contract Republic delivered over 600 sets and spares and was twice the recipient of the Boeing 'Pride in Excellence' award. The 747 programme did represent a long-term, profitable contract, and production continued for twenty years until 1987 when all operations ceased. Similarly, between 1982 and 1987 Republic built the main landing gear doors and fairings for the gigantic Lockheed C-5B transport. Each of the doors and fairings was 69ft long and weighed 5,000lb, and over fifty such assemblies were delivered.

Terrapin and 'Dyna-Soar'

During the 1960s Republic was fairly heavily involved in the burgeoning US space programme, which the company had correctly identified as the next major area of interest in aerospace at an early stage. Republic's first non-military missile was the Terrapin. Developed in the mid-1950s, this was a high-altitude research and weather-reconnaissance

Above: In the late 1960s Republic was due to build the tail sections for the Boeing SST. However, Congress terminated the project following budgetary and environmental concerns. Right: Republic's first venture into the spaceflight field was the Terrapin scientific sounding rocket of the mid-1950s. With a maximum altitude of over 80 miles, the 15ft long, two-stage Terrapin gathered important information on the Earth's upper atmosphere.

Left: In 1958, wanting to build a firm foundation for future spaceflight investigations and contracts, Republic initiated a multi-million dollar expansion of its research and development facilities, the focal point of which was the new Paul Moore Research Center. This became one of the best-equipped private space research facilities in the country.

rocket developed in conjunction with the University of Maryland and named after the University's mascot, a turtle. It was a light-weight, low-cost, high-performance vehicle, and on its first firing, in July 1956 from Wallops Island, Virginia, it raced 80 miles skywards at a peak speed of 3,800mph, sending back scientific data by radio. A solid-propellant rocket motor fired Terrapin to 10,000ft in approximately six seconds at 1,900mph, at which altitude the first stage of the rocket separated from the second stage, which coasted another 30,000ft higher; then the second-stage motor shot Terrapin to 50,000ft at Mach 5.8 and the rocket coasted the rest of the way to peak altitude. Carrying 6lb of scientific instruments, it took only 5.6min to complete a mission.

Both the missile, which was 15ft long and 6in wide and weighed only 224lb, and its collap-sible, zero-length launcher could be transported in a standard-size US station wagon, while three men could easily set it up and fire it. Costing less than the fins of larger scientific rockets, Terrapin was used by the university of Maryland to obtain data that was analyzed to formulate an integrated picture of the Earth's upper atmosphere. It thus gathered the information about cosmic rays and upper air temperatures which was necessary in order properly to plan future spacecraft. Republic produced a small quan-tity of Terrapins until 1957.

Wanting to build a firm foundation for future spaceflight investigations and contracts, in 1958 Republic initiated a multi-million dollar expansion of its research and development

facilities, the focal point of which was its new Paul Moore Research and Development Center. This became one of the best-equipped private space research facilities in the country. Housing eight laboratories – Space Environment and Life Sciences, Re-Entry Simulation, Materials Development, Nuclear Radiation, Guidance and Controls Systems, Electronics, Fluid Systems and Wind Tunnels – the new centre served as the integrating force behind the company's research into advanced aeronautics, missiles, and astronautics; in addtion, each of the laboratries was a self-sustaining unit capable of solving a particular set of space-age problems within its own area of specialization. With the completion of the Center in 1960 –

Below: One of the first projects undertaken at the Paul Moore Center was the design of an orbital bomber under the US Air Force's 'Dyna-Soar' programme. The programme was ultimately cancelled by Congress.

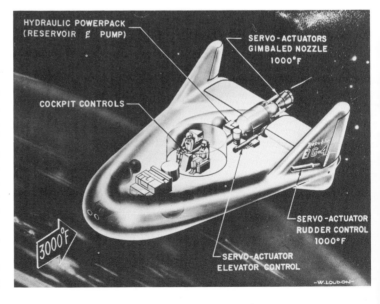

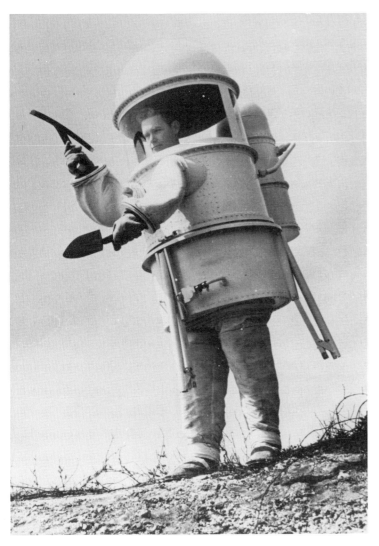

Above: Republic's first NASA contract was awarded in 1960 – that for the design and construction of a prototype Lunar Exploration spacesuit. Republic's unique suit was not intended for actual lunar use but rather to gather practical information on what would and would not work on an actual suit. In this capacity it was a historic and direct ancestor of the Apollo EVA spacesuit used successfully in the late 1960s and early 1970s.

hypersonic research aircraft leading to the development of an orbital bomber and on 1 January 1958 distributed Requests for Proposals to thirteen selected aeorspace contractors, including Republic, for the construction of a 'Dyna-Soar' (Dynamic Soaring) spacecraft. Republic was one of nine companies to respond, offering a two-man, delta-winged, 16,000lb missile; essentially, this was an armed space glider that would be launched by a new three-stage, solid-propellant booster. In June 1958 the Air Force announced that Boeing and Martin were the finalists in the Dyna-Soar competition, but Republic was not to be deterred.

Republic's first space contract was awarded by the National Aeronautics and Space Administration (NASA) in 1960, to design and develop a prototype Lunar Exploration spacesuit; this was the first contract NASA ever awarded for such an item. In response Republic developed a unique spacesuit comprising a cylindrical body and domed top with flexible, pressurized arms and legs. The suit also featured tripod telescoping supports to keep it upright when not in use, and to allow the astronaut to tuck up his legs and take the weight off them while resting. The astronaut would have had excellent visibility through a large wrap-around window in the cylinder, and he would have carried a large oxygen canister on his back. Republic engineers tested the suit on a simulated lunar surface in 1960–61 and presumably gathered important information as to what NASA should and should not consider when developing future lunar spacesuits. The 1960 Republic Lunar Space-suit can therefore claim to be a direct ancestor of the Apollo EVA spacesuit worn by astronaut Neil Armstrong in 1969 when he made the historic first step on the Moon.

Project 'Fire'

The first major NASA space contract awarded to Republic covered the design and production of two Project 'Fire' spacecraft, the company being selected from a total of eight manufacturers bidding for the $5 million order. 'Fire' was a Langley Research Center programme designed to obtain research data during atmospheric re-entry at hyperbolic velocities. Essentially, Republic's spacecraft had the same configuration as the Project Apollo Command Module (which was to carry three astronauts) but was smaller, weighing only 185lb. The main purpose of 'Fire' was to

and with the activities of its eight-year-old Missile Systems Division at Hicksville – Republic felt that it had fully equipped itself to meet the challenges of the Space Age. Between 1952 and 1962 the company invested more than $38 million in research and development and acquired the tools necessary to cope with the technical problems of designing advanced aircraft and space vehicles, but in addition to the $14 million Paul Moore Center the company also put into operation, in 1963, a $2½ million space engine research and development laboratory, one of the most advanced facilities devoted to energy conversion then in existence.

One of the first design projects undertaken at the Paul Moore Center was to research and develop an ancestor of the Space Shuttle. In 1957 the Air Force set up a programme for a

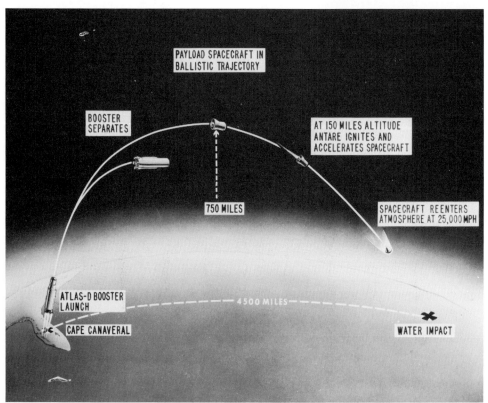

PAYLOAD SPACECRAFT IN BALLISTIC TRAJECTORY

BOOSTER SEPARATES

AT 150 MILES ALTITUDE ANTARE IGNITES AND ACCELERATES SPACECRAFT

750 MILES

SPACECRAFT REENTERS ATMOSPHERE AT 25,000 MPH

ATLAS-D BOOSTER LAUNCH

CAPE CANAVERAL

4500 MILES

WATER IMPACT

Left: From launch, the 'Fire' spacecraft followed a ballistic trajectory over the Atlantic, landing some 4,500 miles down-range. Its maximum altitude was almost 750 miles and no attempt was made at recovery. The 'Fire' spacecraft's performance was excellent, gathering all the data necessary for the successful use of the Apollo Command Module during the lunar landing missions.

Far left: The 'Fire' spacecraft, probably Republic's most important space contract, under construction in 1963. The small, 185lb spacecraft was essentially a miniature Apollo Command Module designed to test the validity of the actual Module's shape and heatshield during re-entry at lunar return speeds.
Left: Loading the completed Republic 'Fire' spacecraft into the nose of an Atlas Missile. The manned Apollo Command Module could not be flown until the results of the 'Fire' flights were known.
Far right: The 'Fire' spacecraft as it appeared during re-entry. Two spacecraft were launched in 1964 and 1965, instrumentation on board continuously transmitting information on stability, heating and communication through-out the 32min flights.

demonstrate the stability of the Apollo CM shape and to test the proposed heat-shield at lunar return speeds.

The major experiments aboard 'Fire' were concerned with the measurement of total spacecraft heating and its radiative heating, radio signal attenuation (communication before, during and after the 'blackout' period), materials behaviour during actual re-entry (testing how the ablative Apollo CM heatshield of beryllium and phenolic asbestos held up during re-entry at lunar return speeds) and Re-entry Package Motion (testing the Apollo CM's stability and determining the best angle of attack); thus 'Fire' was to gather the important data required for the future design of the necessary protective systems for manned lunar and planetary spacecraft to ensure their safe return to Earth.

In April 1964 and May 1965 two Republic 'Fire' spacecraft were launched on Atlas D boosters from Cape Canaveral over the Atlantic Missile Range. From launch, the spacecraft followed a ballistic path over the Atlantic, landing 4,500 miles down range. After launch and separation, the 'Fire' spacecraft coasted for 21min up to a maximum altitude of 500 miles; on the way down, on its parabolic flight, at an altitude of 186 miles an Antares rocket motor was ignited to boost 'Fire' up to 25,000mph – the anticipated lunar return speed for the Apollo Command Module. 'Fire' was monitored for the duration of its 32min flight and no attempt was made at recovery. Instrumentation on board the craft transmitted research data on temperature, pressure, communications and stability to ground receiving stations via two telemetry links, shedding new scientific light on heating rates, radio signal 'blackout' and materials performance during the 25,000mph re-entry. In all, the performance of the 'Fire' re-entry package was excellent, all the required data which led to the successful development and use of the Apollo Command Module being gathered; according to NASA, 'All flight objectives were accomplished'.

Following their winning of the 'Fire' contract, Republic were awarded several more contracts for space projects in rapid succession. In the early 1960s the company won a contract from the Air Force to develop fasteners – rivets, bolts and other mechanical devices needed in spacecraft construction – that could withstand the stresses of space

flight. Simultaneously, the Moore Center was designing a proposed Lunar Orbiting Spacecraft which would carry three astronauts on a fourteen-day reconnaissance of the Moon. Similar in size and shape to the Apollo Command Module as later built by North American, Republic's version got just past the mock-up stage when the production contract was awarded to its competitor.

MOL and AOSO

In 1964 Republic won a contract to design and build the interior for the Air Force's Manned Orbiting Laboratory. MOL was to be a 10ft-diameter, 26ft-long structure which was to be placed in orbit by Titan III for an extended period in 1967. A two-man Gemini spacecraft was to be attached to the end of the laboratory for accommodating the astronauts during launch and re-entry. The laboratory was to be pressurized to permit crew members to operate in a 'shirt-sleeve environment' and experiments were to be conducted to assess man's ability to operate in zero-gravity and perform useful missions in space. For MOL, Republic was to build the living quarters. However, in 1968 Congress terminated MOL as

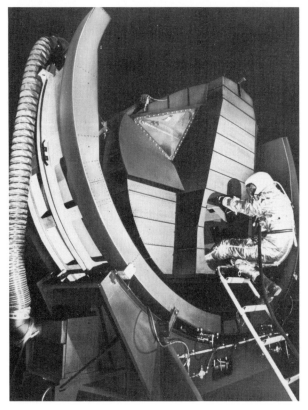

Far left: Republic's proposal for a three-man, fourteen-day lunar orbiting spacecraft – an unsuccessful competitor for the Rockwell Apollo Command Module.
Left: In the mid 1960s Republic was contracted to build the interior of the Air Force's Manned Orbiting Laboratory (MOL). This full-scale mock-up was produced at the factory but the programme itself was cancelled.

an unnecessary duplication of NASA's plans for an orbiting space station.

The major American space programme of the 1960s was Project Apollo, and in this, too, Republic played a role: in September 1962 it was one of nine companies bidding to build the Lunar Module, the contract for which was ultimately awarded to Grumman. The major difference between Republic's and Grumman's proposals was that the former was to use the same rocket engine for lunar landing and lift-off, whereas the latter employed two separate engines. In spite of losing the LM contract, Republic was awarded the contract to build the Lunar Module Docking Trainer which was ultimately sent to the Manned Spacecraft Center in Houston for training astronauts. The Trainer enabled the Apollo astronauts to simulate the docking manoeuvre which they later performed in lunar orbit.

Republic's first and only satellite was the Advanced Orbiting Solar Observatory, built in 1964–65. In April 1964 Republic received a contract from NASA for the development of a second-generation scientific satellite, to be built in order to fill a vast gap in the understanding of solar phenomena, specific-

ally high-radiation solar flares, which could cause a radiation hazard to space flight as well as affecting radio transmissions. The 1,450lb AOSO satellite was placed in a near-polar orbit at a 300-mile altitude in order to be outside the disturbing influences of the Earth's atmosphere. Equipped with eight solar panels and scientific instruments, the spacecraft measured solar activity in ultraviolet, X- and Gamma rays, the observations being stored in a tape recorder and telemetered to the ground stations on command. The satellite was built for NASA's Goddard Spaceflight Center and was successfully launched by a Thor Agena B rocket from Vandenburg Air Force Base, California, in 1966.

In 1964 Republic also won a NASA contract to define Extra-Vehicular Activity (EVA) procedures and techniques to optimize the performance of astronauts in support of manned space operations; the company was also to define the concepts for space structures requiring astronaut EVA support. To this end, engineers in spacesuits, hanging from a crane, deployed and experimented with various cantilevered structures which would be folded for compactness during launching, tightening them and then attaching

Far left: Republic did build the docking simulator for the Apollo Lunar Module. Essentially the front of the Ascent Stage in a moving rig, it trained astronauts for future missions.
Left: Republic's only satellite, the Advanced Orbiting Solar Observatory (AOSO), seen here, almost complete, under test. AOSO was to study various solar phenomena which could be hazardous to spaceflight.
Right: AOSO under construction, in 1965. The 1,500lb satellite was placed in a polar orbit.

reflective material such as could be used for a large antenna. Large deployable structures like these are still planned for the US Space Station which is to be launched in the mid-1990s.

In the late 1960s Republic won a most unusual contract, that for designing and building a toilet for the US Skylab space station. The $17 million contract for the waste managment system (nicknamed 'Astrojohn') led to an effective, zero-maintenance device that was extensively tested by Republic in both gravity and zero-gravity situations. The space toilet, America's first ever, had to compact and contain human waste and demonstrate zero-G collection, non-manual collection, the total deactivation of microbiological matter, sealed disposal, the total containment of products of disposal from the cabin environment, and physiological acceptability. The waste management system as developed by Republic was installed in Skylab and was successfully used during several long-duration missions in 1973–74, working flawlessly in space for 531 days.

Scramjet and Shuttle

Beginning in the 1950s, Republic's visionary engineer Alexander Kartveli hired the Italian ramjet pioneer Antonio Ferri (considered the father of hypersonic propulsion) to assist in the development of the XF-103's engines. After the XF-103 programme ended, Kartveli urged the development of 'the ultimate airplane', an ascent-to-orbit aircraft. Thus, beginning in 1961, Republic started the basic research on what came to be called the 'aerospaceplane'. Ferri was kept on the payroll as a consultant in the project, working on controlling the high temperature of combustion by maintaining a supersonic air flow through the engine. Republic's early 1960s design clearly foreshadowed the design for the US National Aerospaceplane (X-30) of the 1990s.

Foreseeing the need for such a future reusable spacecraft, in 1964 NASA awarded Republic several study contracts for hypersonic 'scramjet' vehicles. The scramjet was to be a safe, cost-efficient, single-stage-to-orbit craft with a unique rocket engine that was also air-breathing within the Earth's atmosphere. In response, a large, 116,500lb reusable winged spacecraft was designed, its 28,000lb payload far larger than that of any spacecraft then in use. The craft could be flown manned or unmanned. Although this scramjet was never built, the United States is planning a new version which will be test-flown in the mid-1990s.

The development of electrical propulsion for spacecraft and satellite control – a field which Republic pioneered – was undertaken at the Paul Moore Center, with work concentrating on the preparation for flight-test of experimental 'pinch-plasma' engines; such engines were not used for lift-off power but rather to change the attitude or direction of vehicles once they were in orbit and for maintaining their position in space. Work started at the company in 1957 as an in-house project and resulted in a 1961 contract for satellite thrusters. The unique pulsed-plasma rocket engines as developed by Republic were simple, battery-powered, solid-fuel systems. The solid propellant eliminated the need for tankage, valves and feedlines and was unaffected by G forces and radiation. The motors had an instant start/stop capability, with an extremely short impulse duration, and Republic's designs were the only electrical propulsion systems with thrust-throttling. They were very simple motors, reliable in that

Below: In 1964 Republic won another NASA contract, to define Extra-Vehicular Activity (EVA) procedures and techniques to optimize the performance of astronauts in support of manned space operations.
Right: The zero-gravity space toilet, 'Astrojohn', built by Republic for the Skylab space station.
Far right: In the early 1970s, NASA Center Director Wehrner von Braun (seen here seated) visited Republic and 'tried out' one of the Space Toilet concepts.
Below right: Throughout the 1960s Republic was working to define a single-stage-to-orbit hypersonic scramjet spacecraft for NASA.
Below far right: In the early 1960s Republic developed 'pinch-plasma' electrical propulsion systems for spacecraft.

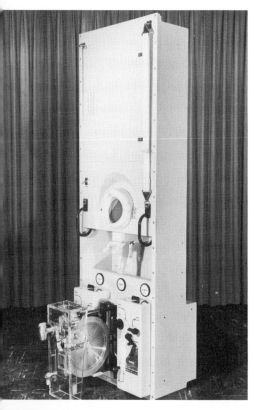

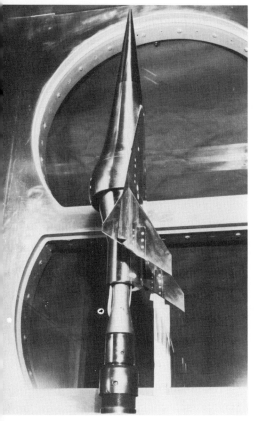

Left: Republic's last (and possibly most important) space contract was to build the vertical fin and rudder for the Space Shuttle orbiter. Between 1973 and 1984 a total of six sets were assembled, all of which performed flawlessly on many missions. The Shuttle's vertical stabilizer and rudder provides critical directional control and velocity management during atmospheric flight and landing. Here Republic workers assemble the rudder hinge area.
Below left: Upon landing, the Shuttle rudder splits vertically in half, as shown here, to operate as a speed brake.

they had virtually no moving parts. Republic's motors were flown on one satellite, the Air Force's LES-6 which was launched in September 1968. This satellite had four thrusters which generated four micro-pounds of thrust, enabling it to perform east/west station-keeping in a relay capacity.

Republic's last space contract, awarded in 1973, was for the design, tooling and fabrication of the Space Shuttle Orbiter's vertical tail; for this project Republic was a subcontractor to Rockwell International. The Shuttle vertical stabilizer, which includes the rudder, provides directional control and velocity management during atmospheric flight and landing. Upon landing, the rudder splits vertically in half to operate as a speed brake. The primary structure of the tail was optimized for minimum weight, with integrally stiffened, machined aluminium skins and

Far right: One of Republic's Shuttle tails upon completion. The vertical tail has to be extremely strong to withstand the stress of launch and re-entry and rigid enough to ensure that none of the surface insulation tiles spring off. Below: Every Space Shuttle that has flown has had a Republic tail on it: the legacy of the makers of the P-47 flies on.

featuring the extensive use of adhesive-bonded honeycomb sandwich panels. The Shuttle tail has to be extremely strong, able to withstand the critical acoustic environment of up to 156db during launch and the critical thermal environment during re-entry; it must also provide a buckle-free exterior skin for interface with bonded re-usable surface insulation tiles. A total of six units were constructed by Republic between 1973 and 1984 and these have all been used successfully on many orbital missions.

The last space contracts under investigation by Republic were for the future US Space Station, sheduled to be launched in 1996. These included food systems studies, housekeeping systems, sanitation agents and the Space Station waste management system, drawing on Skylab experience. However, Republic ceased operations before any new hardware was actually constructed.

Republic in the Modern Era

A T THE END of 1964 production at Republic ground to a halt. The F-105 programme fell victim to the idealistic, and nearly disastrous, McNamara concept of 'commonality' among service fighters and was thus terminated. Republic then lacked any major airframe contract to pick up the slack, and on the major subcontract work it had in hand – fabricating the aft fuselage for the McDonnell F-4 fighter – it was losing money. Employment dropped to 8,000 and the future looked bleak.

Then in 1965 the Fairchild Corporation of Hagerstown, Maryland, purchased the operating assests of Republic Aviation and the latter became a Division. This was not a hostile take-over, as Fairchild apparently hoped to revive the ailing Farmingdale company; moreover, had it not been for the take-over, Republic probably would have ceased all operations in 1965. Fairchild then installed its own President and set in train a programme to pare costs and consolidate facilities. The Paul Moore Center was closed and much of the equipment and large numbers of personnel were shipped to Maryland though many of its engineers left the company to travel to nearby Grumman. The closure marked, in effect, the end of long-term R&D at Republic. The number of employees was further reduced to 3,700 and for 1964 Republic lost $3 million. Furthermore, the company still had no new aircraft to build.

VTOL fighter

Hopes were raised in 1966 when Fairchild-Republic won a contract, over three leading US airframe manufacturers, to build an advanced new vertical take-off and landing (VTOL) tactical fighter for the Air Force. Republic's engineers had been working on this proposal for some time and the win seemed to put the company back in the forefront of advanced

military fighter technology. The project was a collaborative one involving the United States and the Federal Republic of Germany, Entwicklungsring Sud (EWR) being the partners.

The design featured retractable engines located just forward of the variable-sweep wings and vectored thrust lift-cruise engines in the rear, and although the aircraft would have been lighter and more manoeuvrable than the F-105 it could have carried greater payloads. The V/STOL capability was seen as being necessary in Europe, allowing operations from bomb-damaged runways.

The retractable lift engines, when deployed, could have been tilted to varying degrees from the horizontal to provide vertical lift or a short take-off capability. The aircraft would also have featured a new type of General Electric trubofan engine with twice the thrust-to-weight ratio of other jet engines. Initially, Republic and EWR were jointly funded to the tune of $6 million by the two governments and it was anticipated that the

Above: The end of an era: Alexander Kartveli (left) nearing retirement from Republic in the late 1960s yet still designing advanced aircraft. From this mind sprang the designs of everything from the P-35 to an advanced supersonic fighter (model in foreground).

go-ahead for a prototype programme would begin early in 1967. This schedule would have called for the manufacture of twelve aircraft at a cost of $500 million by the end of 1971, and if the aircraft went into full production in 1972–73 the programme had the potential for becoming the largest for fighter aircraft in US history. However, in February 1968, after a period of wavering, the US decided not to proceed with the fighter as Defense Secretary McNamara saw no clear need for such an aircraft. This decision effectively ended the programme as Germany could not afford to fund the development on its own.

If Republic's V/STOL fighter had been built it would have had a length of 64ft 6in and a wing span of 29ft minimum and 47ft maximum. Its speed would have been Mach 1.5 and its range over 3,000 miles, while its armament would have comprised an M-61 20mm cannon plus nuclear or conventional ordnance.

F-15 proposal

After the cancellation of the US/FRG fighter Republic attempted to translate the research experience into the design of a V/STOL business jet or commuter airliner – the company's third attempt to get into the airline market following the Rainbow and the abortive project for the RC-4 turboprop airliner in the late 1950s. Republic's proposed FH-V1 was a fourteen-passenger aircraft featuring four GE J85 engines, two wing-mounted for lift and two fuselage-mounted for cruise. It would have been 66ft long, with a 46ft wing span and a cruising range of 1,000 miles, and its speed would have been Mach 0.8 at 40,000ft. The FH-V2 business jet was smaller, 50ft long, and would have been powered by three J85s, one main fuselage lift fan and two deployable fuselage lift/cruise fans. It would have carried seven passengers plus two crewmen. Nothing became of either project.

The years 1968–69 marked a turning point in the history of the corporation. With no new aircraft in production, the engineering staff spent their time formulating detailed proposals for the Air Force's new air superiority fighter, then designated F-X and later F-15. Intended to replace the F-4, this was clearly going to be the Air Force's last new fighter programme for a long time, and in early 1969 Republic was buoyed by its selection as one of three finalists for the project, the others being Rockwell and McDonnell Douglas.

The Republic F-15 proposal featured two engines in widely separated nacelles and a fixed, cranked wing, the company's design group having begun to investigate the concept of separating the engines in podded nacelles ('three-body concept') because of the known difficulties experienced in the installation of

Right: The highly advanced swing-wing US/FRG VTOL fighter concept. Republic began co-development of this aircraft in the mid-1960s, only to see the project cancelled. Two engines in the rear provided cruise propulsion and four lift engines swung out from the fuselage.

high-performance engines in the fuselage where unfavourable flow disturbances adversely affected the efficiency of the powerplants. This consideration, plus the promise of reduced wave and aft-end drag at high speed, provided the initial impetus; however, it was soon evident that this unique design also offered sizable savings in weight because of its inherently efficient structural arrangement. Lessons in survivability learned from the F-105's combat experience in Vietnam were also applied to the new design. By separating the engines and housing them in pods, for example, the aircraft's chances of survival were markedly increased in three key areas – through having completely separated and redundant primary controls and control surfaces, by locating the fuel tanks well away from the hot sections of the engines and by introducing true twin-engine reliability. The costs for the future development of the aircraft could also be reduced because the three-body concept could accept changes in engine dimensions with minimal disruption to the structural arrangement, while savings were also possible because the F-15 design lent itself to simple sub-assemblies. The Republic F-15 would have had a length of 65ft 5in and a wing span of 38ft 11in. Its speed would have been in excess of Mach 2 and its range over 3,000 miles. Power was to come from two F100 turbofan engines and the aircraft's armament would have comprised air-to-air missiles, an M-61 20mm cannon and up to 16,000lb of external ordnance.

In late 1969, however, McDonnell Douglas, in a highly controversial and politicized decision, was selected to build the F-15. Republic had devoted an intensive effort to the programme and had, without question, offered an outstanding design, but it is often the case that design considerations alone do not decide which manufacturer will build a particular aircraft. To date, McDonnell Douglas has produced over 1,000 F-15s and, twenty years on, it is still in production – a remarkably long life for a fighter aircraft. Had Republic won this contract, the company would probably still be building F-15s today.

There were, evidently, several obscure reasons why Republic lost the F-15 contract. First, there is no question that McDonnell Douglas had a stronger political lobby. Second, it was rumoured that, several months before the contract was awarded, the FBI traced a major leak of information directly

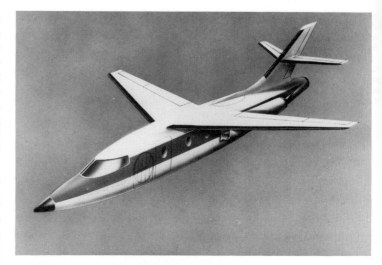

from Republic's F-15 programme to the Israeli Consulate in New York and thus a number of Air Force generals may have been ill disposed towards Republic on grounds of security. Finally, weeks before the F-15 decision was announced, Grumman won the contract to build the air superiority F-14 fighter for the Navy, and for geo-political reasons it is doubtful that the Pentagon would have awarded two major aircraft contracts to corporations whose principal factories were but nine miles apart.

The A-10 Thunderbolt II

Following the loss of the F-15 contract Republic concentrated its engineering efforts on another forthcoming Air Force contract, that for a new close air support aircraft – the first USAF machine to be designed specifically for the role. In April 1970 the Deputy Secretary of Defense approved the A-X (Attack Experimental) aircraft for competitive prototype

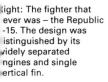

development, and a month later the Air Force issued formal Requests for Proposals to twelve airframe contractors inviting A-X tenders. In December 1970 the Northrop Corporation and Fairchild-Republic were selected as finalists to participate in the competitive develop-ment of prototypes.

The Northrop aircraft was designated A-9 and the Republic entry A-10, each company being paid $41 million to design and build two prototypes which would then compete in a 'fly-off'. Following the first flights in May 1972, each contractor conducted an extensive test programme prior to turning the aircraft over to the Air Force that October, whereupon pilots from both the developing command (Air Force Systems Command) and the user command (Tactical Air Command) flew the prototypes until December 1972, completing 635 hours of competitive trials. The contract for 720 A-10s was expected to be worth $1.5 billion.

In January 1973 the Secretary of the Air Force announced that the Republic A-10 prototype had been selected for full-scale development and in March the company was awarded a contract, worth $159 million, to build ten aircraft, to develop fully the weapon system and to continue prototype flight-testing. The victory in the A-10 competition ended a ten-year quest by the company for a prime contract involving a major aircraft programme, and as production continued in the mid-1970s of F-14 tails, F-4 tails and

Boeing 747 control surfaces, profits soared by 60 per cent and employment reached 5,500. The first development A-10 was delivered in 1975; and by 1976 production stood at 75 aircraft a year, increasing to 120 in 1977.

The A-10, now named the Thunderbolt II, was designed for the accurate delivery of ordnance at low altitude and high speed. Equipped with missiles, bombs and a 30mm 'Gatling' type cannon, it was intended to counter Soviet armour in Europe. It would be able to survive intense anti-aircraft fire thanks to its armour plating, redundant systems and separated engines. The provision of effective anti-armour support for ground forces in a high-threat air defence environment called for a unique aircraft: it had to be deadly against tanks and other targets; it had to be able to carry large ordnance payloads and elec-tronic and infra-red countermeasures simul-taneously and have excellent range and long loiter capabilities near the battle area; it had to be able to fly and manoeuvre at very low altitudes and to survive intense anti-aircraft fire, surface-to-air missiles and attacks by other aircraft; and, finally, it had to be able to maintain high sortie rates and operate from short fields, while permitting rapid servicing and easy repair of battle damage.

The A-10 features a low-set cantilever wing with a thick, high-lift aerofoil, made of aluminium alloy and with a one-piece, constant-chord centre-section. The outer

Left: The first YA-10A is rolled out of Republic's factory, spring 1972. This was one of the aircraft that competed in the 'fly-off' against the Northrop A-9.

Right: A-10 engine build-up. The engines will be installed inside the high-set nacelle pods.

Left: The first prototype A-10, now loaded with bombs, photographed while based at Edwards, October 1972.

DROP STATION
A10A
ENGINE BUILD-UP

Left: The first production A-10, now named the 'Thunderbolt II', is rolled out of Republic's Farmingdale plant, October 1975.

Right: The A-10 assembly line in Republic's Building 17 — exactly the same site as that of the former P-47 assembly line.

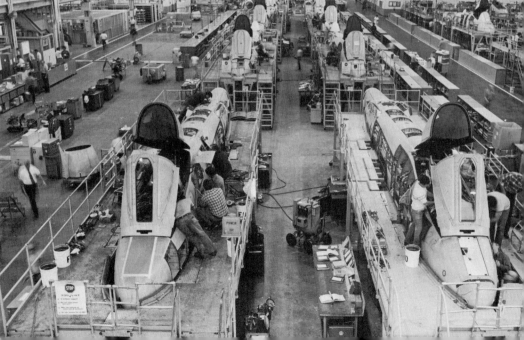

Left: The A-10 can carry up to eight tons of ordnance specifically intended for close air support – mainly to destroy enemy armour. Pictured are the electronic counter-measures pods, Maverick TV-guided missiles, Paveway laser-guided bombs and 1,350 rounds of 30mm ammunition.
Right: An inboard profile of the A-10 reveals the location of the cannon, ammunition drum, fuel tanks and titanium armour 'bath-tub' surrounding the pilot.

panels taper and have 7 degrees of dihedral. It features integrally stiffened skins with drooped wing tips and single-slotted Fowler flaps, and the ailerons, for high manoeuvrability, are made up of dual upper and lower surfaces that separate to serve as air brakes. The fuselage is a simple, semi-monocoque structure of aluminium alloy with a mimimum of compound curves for ease of manufacture and repair. The constant-chord tailplane is a cantilever aluminium alloy structure with twin fins and interchangeable rudders mounted at the tips. The landing gear is a retractable tricycle type with single wheels on each unit. Interchangeable main wheel units retract into non-structural pod fairings attached to the lower surfaces of the wings, the wheels partially protruding when retracted (as in the P-35) as drag is not a factor; the nosewheel is distinc-tively offset to starboard to keep the nose-mounted gun on the centreline. The A-10's cockpit is located well forward of the wings and features a large 'bubble' canopy to provide all-around visibility. It is equipped with a bulletproof windscreen and the canopy hinges at the rear, while the pilot's ACES II zero/zero ejection seat is operable at speeds of up to 510mph.

The A-10 has an unmatched capability for high sortie rates, low maintenance require-ments and rapid battle damage repair. Its ability to loiter for hours within the battle area operating at altitudes of less than 1,000ft and

with visibility of only one mile makes it highly responsive to the immediate needs of the ground combat commander, while the aircraft's short take-off and landing capability permits sorties in and out of forward operating locations. Mounted internally along the aircraft's centreline is the GAU-8/A 30mm Gatling gun system, a weapon designed to defeat the full array of ground targets encountered in close air support. The A-10 can carry up to 16,000lb of mixed ordnance on eleven pylon stations, including both con-ventional and laser guided weapons, rockets, cluster bomb munitions, Maverick missiles, electronic countermeasures equipment and internal flare and chaff dispensers. Once the pilot has locked a Maverick on a target he can

Above: An A-10 mounting six Mk 82 500lb bombs.
Right: Early production A-10s, in two-tone grey camouflage, assigned to the 354th TFW, Myrtle Beach AFB, South Carolina, 1976. The scoop under the nose gun is for gun compartment venting.

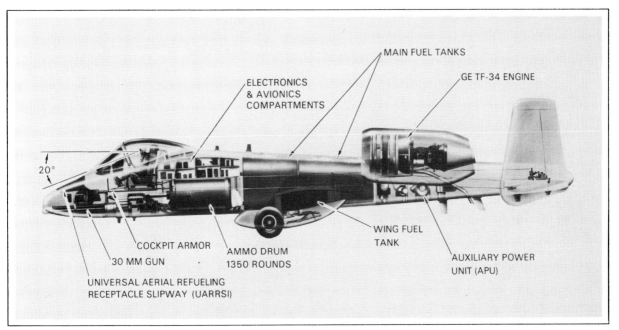

MAIN FUEL TANKS

GE TF-34 ENGINE

ELECTRONICS
& AVIONICS
COMPARTMENTS

20°

COCKPIT ARMOR

30 MM GUN

UNIVERSAL AERIAL REFUELING
RECEPTACLE SLIPWAY (UARRSI)

AMMO DRUM
1350 ROUNDS

WING FUEL
TANK

AUXILIARY POWER
UNIT (APU)

'fire and forget'; the Maverick will then track and strike the target whether it is stationary or moving.

Simplicity and survivability

Everything about the A-10 was designed for simplicity. All the major components are located close to the ground level and access doors are large. Its structure is conventional, approximately 95 per cent of the airframe being constructed from aluminium. Single curvature skins are used on all areas aft of the cockpit, permitting ease of maintenance, while redundant load paths are used throughout the aircraft for extra reliability and damage tolerance. Numerous parts are interchangeable left and right, including the engine, main landing gear and vertical stabilizers.

As an A-10 in combat would be a target for every gun and missile in the area, the goal in designing the aircraft was to provide survivability against a single direct hit. It achieves this through a combination of high manoeuvrability at low air-speeds and altitudes and an inbuilt resistance to damage. The pilot, for example, is protected by a $^3/_4$-ton, 1in thick titanium 'bath-tub' which also protects the vital element of the flight control system. This armoured 'bath-tub' is capable of withstanding hits by projectiles up to 23mm in calibre. Redundant primary structural elements can survive major damage; fuel is contained in four independent, self-sealing fuel cells which are protected with internal and external foam; separated and shielded flight controls are triple-redundant; the engines are widely spaced; and the primary redundant hydraulic flight control system is further enhanced by a cable back-up 'manual reversion' system which permits the pilot to fly and land the aircraft when all hydraulics are lost. In all, one out of every eight pounds of the A-10's weight has been engineered specifically for survivability – even the 30mm ammunition drum is protected by two layers of armour plating. In survivability tests one A-10 was riddled with over 700 rounds of 23mm armour-piercing incendiary and high-explosive without sustaining critical damage. However, it should be noted that the Thunderbolt II was designed before the proliferation of cheap, simple, shoulder-fired missiles that so aggravated Soviet air operations in Afghanistan.

The avionics subsystem for the A-10 is composed of communication/navigation/identification equipment and penetration aids. The communication/navigation/identification equipment comprises UHF/AM, VHF/AM and VHF/FM radios, tacan, IFF, VHF/ADF, an X-band beacon, an Instrument Landing

Right: More A-10s at Myrtle Beach. Note the many external stores pylons and also the flaps in the landing position. The shape of the fin differs from that on the prototypes.

System (ILS) and a flight director computer. The fire control/weapons delivery equipment is a fairly new development and consists of a head-up display (HUD), a TV monitor and control, an Armament Control System and the Pave Penny laser search/track set. Penetration aids include the radar warning receiver (RWR), the internal flare/chaff dispensing system and ECM pods. The majority of the avionics subsystems, except for the HUD, TV monitor, Armament Control System and Pave Penny pod, are located in the avionics bays aft of the cockpit on both the port and starboard sides

of the aircraft. The HUD subsystem is located forward of the instrument panel and presents essential information on a projected-image screen in the pilot's forward field of vision; the TV monitor and Armament Control system are on the main instrument panel; and the Pave Penny pod hangs below the starboard side of the fuselage aft of the nose landing gear.

No attack aircraft has ever mounted a gun with the tank-killing capability of the GAU-8/A in a single strafing pass. In addition to the armour-piercing projectile, which is capable of penetrating medium and heavy tanks, the gun

Far left: The generally uncluttered main instrument panel of the A-10. The control column is visible in the centre, the throttle on the left side and the head-up display at top centre.
Left: The roomy and high-set A-10 cockpit (giving the pilot a good view of the battlefield) is equipped with a McDonnell Douglas ACES II ejection seat. Note the upward-rising canopy, and the canopy breakers on top of the ejection seat.
Right: The fuselages of two A-10s, Nos. 111 and 112, have their skin riveted on at Farmingdale. Note the three-piece wings taking shape at the rear.

fires high-explosive incendiary ammunition which is extremely effective against a wide variety of 'softer' targets. The weapon is mounted on the aircraft's centreline for ease of aiming and to create a stable, accurate platform. It is a conventional gun with seven rotating barrels and is supplied with ammunition from a linkless feed and storage system holding 1,350 rounds. The acquisition of a revolutionary new ammunition loading system has been the major contributor in reducing aircraft turnaround time from three hours to about fifteen minutes between wartime sorties. The total weight of the gun system is 4,029lb and the rate of fire is 2,100 or 4,200 rounds a minute.

The A-10 is powered by two quiet, smokeless General Electric TF34-100 engines, each generating over 9,000lb of thrust. The TF34-100 is a dual-spool, high-bypass-ratio turbofan, in the design of which ruggedness, reliability and maintainability were the primary considerations. Modular construction permits quick access to various engine components, while split cowls provide access to gearbox accessories, engine blades and vanes. The engines are enclosed in armoured pods and mounted on pylons to the upper rear fuselage immediately aft of the wing trailing edge to minimize foreign object ingestion. Additional fuel can be carried in three 600 US gallon jettisonable external tanks carried on underwing and fuselage centreline pylons. The A-10 has provision for mounting an in-flight refuelling probe on the upper starboard side of the forward fuselage as well as having a built-in receptacle in the nose; it also features

Left, top: The A-10 was literally designed around the GAU-8/A 'Gatling' gun, which is the size of an automobile. No other aircraft has ever mounted a gun with the tank-killing ability of this weapon.

Left, centre: In 1977 a special operation known as JAWS (Joint Attack Weapons Systems) was conducted at Fort Hunter Liggett, California, to investigate the best methods of employing the A-10 in combat. For these tests the aircraft were painted in a green and brown scheme. This low-flying A-10 demonstrates the aircraft's extreme manoeuvrability.

Left, bottom: A KC-135 refuels an A-10. The refuelling receptacle is located in the aircraft's nose, directly in front of the cockpit, greatly simplifying link-up and station-keeping by the A-10 pilot.

Above right: Most of the A-10's avionics subsystems are located in bays (shown here with access doors open) aft of the cockpit on both sides of the fuselage. The windscreen hinges forward to permit access to the rear of the instrument panel.

Below: An A-10 of the 176th TFS poses in standard 'European I', two-tone green paintwork.

an on-board auxiliary power unit (APU) for quick engine start. The Thunderbolt II is 53ft 4in long and has a wing span of 57ft 6in. Its best speed is over 400mph and it has a range of 2,500 miles.

The first operational A-10 Wing was the 354th TFW, based at Myrtle Beach, South Carolina, to which unit deliveries began in March 1977. The first squadron in Europe to receive the A-10 was the 81st TFW at Bentwaters, England, in early 1979. The 81st, with its six squadrons and some 108 A-10s, was the largest fighter wing in the US Air Force and, indeed, NATO. The aircraft are constantly rotated to four Forward Operating Locations

(FOLs) in Germany, the 510th and 92nd operating out of Sembach and Leipheim in southern Germany and two other squadrons, the 91st and the 78th, from Ahlhorn and Norverich in the northern region. Six squadrons of A-10s are currently based in England, the 92nd and 510th at Bentwaters, the 78th and 91st at Woodbridge and the 509th and 511th at Alconbury, the last pair having moved from the 81st at Bentwaters to form the 10th TFW in May 1988. In the United States, A-10s are assigned to TAC, to the Air Force Reserve and to Air National Guard units; they also operate out of bases in Alaska and South Korea.

Night/Adverse Weather variant

In an effort to improve the effectiveness of the A-10 at night and in poor weather, one of the original single-seat development aircraft was modified by the company into a two-seat Night/Adverse Weather version. Since the original A-10A was designed with future modification to a two-seater variant in mind, the N/AW aircraft retained all the capabilities of the A-10, with unchanged fuel and ordnance capacities; the modifications consisted simply of relocating some equipment, adding the second cockpit and second canopy and raising the height of the fins to offset turbulence caused by the second cockpit. The N/AW A-10 combined avionics for low-altitude penetration and target acquisition, a 'real world' head-up display allowing the pilot to fly the aircraft and conduct tactical operations. The multi-sensor package in the second seat included forward-looking infra-red (FLIR), multi-mode radar, an inertial navigation unit, a radar altimeter for terrain-avoidance steering information and a laser ranger. However, after

Left: A formation of A-10s in 'European I' camouflage. A-10s are expected to be in front-line service in Europe, to provide close air support, until at least the mid-1990s.

Left: The most commonly seen external fitting on the A-10 is the Pave Penny laser search and track system. Mounted on a pylon under the nose, the sensor detects and tracks some of the reflected electromagnetic energy beamed on to a target from a ground-based laser designator, enabling the A-10's weapons to home in accurately.

its first flight in May 1979, and following subsequent testing by the Air Force, no further action was taken to develop the two-seat A-10.

By 1980 the annual production rate of the A-10 had reached a peak of 144 aircraft, and in 1982 it began to fall. However, many at Republic had seen ominous signs earlier in the programme as they believed that the absentee management (Fairchild) was more concerned about profits than about jobs on Long Island – particularly after Fairchild moved half the work on the A-10 to Maryland.

Surprisingly, there was also resistance to the aircraft from the Air Force, mainly because it did not want it: the Air Force's mission was high-altitude air defence, not snooping around trees hunting tanks. Air Force officials and many members of Congress felt that the A-10 should have gone to the Army. Republic's search for foreign sales for the A-10 failed because the company began its overseas marketing campaign too late; nobody wants to buy an aircraft that is going out of production. Thus the 713th and last A-10 rolled off

Right: The scenario Republic planned for: low-flying A-10s streak into combat destroying enemy tanks along the way.
Below: From its inception the A-10 was designed to accommodate a second cockpit without major modification to the airframe and in 1978 one of the pre-series A-10s was converted to two-seat configuration at company expense for the purpose of demonstrating night/adverse weather attack capabilities.

Republic's assembly line in 1984 and there were the immediate and inevitable large-scale lay-offs. However, the A-10 earned $3 billion for the company and was one of its few profitable programmes.

In 1987, after the closure of Republic, the nearby Grumman Corporation purchased the remaining A-10 assets, and enlisted 200 programme engineers, assuring the Bethpage company of winning future contracts to upgrade the A-10. At the time of writing these should include re-engining the aircraft with General Electric F404-400Ds and integrating advanced avionics, including FLIR and a laser ranger. It is expected, though, that during the mid-1990s the A-10 will gradually be phased out in favour of a new strike version of the Fighting Falcon, the A-16.

The SF-340

Seeking to diversify out of the 'boom or bust' world of military manufacturing, Republic began design work in 1980 on a joint venture with Saab of Sweden for a new-generation short-haul turboprop airliner, the SF-340. Republic would produce the wing sets, nacelles and tail surfaces and Saab would build the fuselage. Work was to start in 1982, and a worldwide market of more than 400 aircraft was predicted for the 1990s. This was the first programme in which an aircraft was, from its inception, designed, produced and marketed as an US-European joint venture, and after several abortive attempts Republic was finally in the airliner business. The

product of the two companies was the Saab-Fairchild SF-340, a twin-engined, 34-seat turboprop transport designed to meet the demand for a cost-effective airliner to replace fuel-inefficient turboprops and jets than in serivce.

The SF-340 was designed with the following main objectives in mind: new standards of fuel economy; low-cost maintenance, ensuring minimum 'downtime'; a pleasant, low-noise environment for the passengers; a short-field capability; low external noise levels; and the production of a family of aircraft capable of meeting many passenger, cargo and specialist requirements. The cabin layout was flexible and could be matched to almost any specific-ation: from the normal 34-seat, all-passenger layout the aircraft could be swiftly converted to various passenger-freight combinations, for example fifteen seats and 4,500lb of cargo. The cabin was more than 7ft wide, with three-abreast, airliner-style seating and a fully 6ft high aisle. It featured dual air-conditioning and environmental control systems, and the entire fuselage including the baggage area was pressurized; it was also equipped with a restroom, a coat closet, carry-on luggage space and, optionally, a galley.

The SF-340's primary structure was de-signed for high utilization rates and long service in arduous short-haul conditions, which involved repeated, short flight cycles, frequent take-offs and landings and a considerable proportion of operational service in low-level turbulence. To cater for

Above: The N/AW version was developed to give battlefield commanders an increased operational capability. The second cockpit contained advanced avionics equipment for navigation, terrain avoidance, target acquisition and weapons delivery. However, the Air Force showed little interest in the project.

Right: Republic's first and last production airliner, the turboprop SF-340, sits on the ramp in Farmingdale. Rising production costs and a slow market meant that only about a hundred wing sets were produced by the company, but the aircraft is still in production in Sweden.

this environment the designers worked to proven fail-safe and safe-life criteria, employing dual load-paths, crack-stoppers and low stress levels. Extensive use was made of large panels with bonded stiffeners and doublers.

The aircraft was to be powered by General Electric CT7-5 engines mounted in nacelles integral with the wing; the dual-wheel main landing gear was mounted on the underside of the wing and retracted into the lower half of the nacelles. The CT7-5 turboprop was chosen for its light weight, good maintainability and low fuel consumption. Each drove a Dowty-Rotol hydraulically controlled, constant-speed, four-bladed propeller. The total fuel capacity was 880 US gallons contained in two integral tanks located one in each wing. Operation of the primary control surfaces was achieved without power assistance by conventional control columns and adjustable rudder pedals. Each wing had one single-slotted, externally hinged flap extending from fuselage to aileron.

Right: The SF-340 production line. Republic produced the wings, engine nacelles and vertical and horizontal tail surfaces.

The SF-340 was 64ft 6in long and had a wing span of 70ft 4in, and it had a range of 1,500 miles at over 300mph. Production began in 1981 and the first aircraft was rolled out on 27 October 1982; the maiden flight took place on 25 January 1983 at Linköping, Sweden, only 29 months after development had begun. The first Amercian airline to operate the SF-340 was the regional carrier Comair, which received its first delivery in June 1983; the first European carrier was the Swiss airline Crossair, which ordered ten of the aircraft and recieved its first in early 1984.

Unfortunately, Republic ran into major production problems with the SF-340. First it tried bonding the skin on the wings, and when that did not work it had to resort to the more expensive method of riveting it. Because of engineering oversights, there were such delays in production that, in order to meet the schedule, company employees were still working on the first wing set while it was on the boat to Sweden! The company calculated that aircraft wing set no. 205 would mark the break-even point in the project after all the R&D money had been expended; but only 96 wing sets were produced before production was halted in 1987. The company took a major financial loss ($85 million) on the project, attributed to rising start-up costs and falling sales projections. However, the SF-340 remains in production in Sweden where its manufacture has proved more profitable.

In spite of its financial problems, the late 1970s and early 1980s saw Republic continue design work on several advanced military aircraft projects in the hope of winning future contracts, including a Next-Generation Close Air Support aircraft (a follow-on for the A-10) and an advanced canard supersonic design made mostly of advanced composites and with a night/adverse weather capability. Republic was also studying a Next-Generation Air Superiority Fighter, a follow-on for the F-15. This advanced, delta-winged design featured internal weapon carriage and supersonic cruise yet had STOL performance. It would have made extensive use of composites and would have been available in the mid to late 1990s. Perhaps Republic's most advanced design was long-range Supersonic Cruise Interceptor. This would have been somewhat akin to an updated XF-103, though slower. It would have had a range of 3,000 miles at Mach 1.5 and an internal weapons carriage of multiple long-range air-to-air missiles. It was

intended to defeat the atmospheric threat – high-performance, cruise-missile-launching bombers. It would feature autonomous sensing so that there would have been no dependence on Airborne Warning & Control Systems (AWACS) nor on aerial refuelling. However, because of Republic's demise, these advanced designs will be left for someone else to build.

The T-46

The determined efforts of Fairchild-Republic to secure a US Air Force contract for the Cessna T-37 replacement began in 1977, when its design for a Next Generation Trainer (NGT) was initiated. Although the Request for Proposals was formally issued in 1981, planning for a replacement for the ageing T-37B had been in progress for several years and a number of manufacturers had been seriously involved since 1979. Republic's competitors for the forthcoming trainer contract included the Gulfstream Peregrine, the Vought/VFW Eaglet, the Rockwell Nova and the General Dynamics Model 210. When, on 2 July 1982, Republic was ultimately selected by the Air Force to develop the NGT (T-46A), many observers suspected that this victory could be attributed to the company's desperate position, brought about by the approaching end of A-10 production, and the Services' traditional need to maintain aircraft manufacturing plants as viable operations probably played no small part in the Pentagon's awarding of this contract. Nonetheless, the T-46 saga was to turn into a tale of woe and intrigue.

The Fairchild-Republic company invested a great deal of time and effort in winning the NGT contract. Over 1,200 hours were spent testing various wind-tunnel models, and several radio-controlled scale models were also flown. Hundreds of hours of work were performed on a flight simulator and a full-scale mock-up was constructed to assist in cockpit development and engineering studies; this mock-up was then sent on a promotional tour around the United States, being placed on display at many Air Force bases. But by far the most unusual aspect of Republic's pre-contract work was the construction and flight-testing (40 hours) of a 62 per cent scale manned demonstrator powered by two TRS-18 turbojets and built by the Ames Industrial Corporation of Bohemia, Long Island. The first flight in this aircraft was made on 10 September 1981 at Mojave, California, with Dick Rutan of the Rutan Aircraft Factory – who had acted as the design consultant for the project – at the controls. Although this programme demanded a substantial investment by Fairchild, it produced much useful data on the aircraft's flight characteristics and undoubtedly helped the company in the Air Force's evaluation of the several NGT competitors.

Thus, in July 1982, Republic won its last aircraft contract and the corporation was much relieved that there would be life after the A-10; somewhat ironically, its first contract for the Air Corps was also for trainers (BT-8s), and Republic had not produced such an aircraft since then. Production of the expected 650 aircraft, for $1.5 billion, was to run until 1993

and the NGT would serve the Air Force well into the twenty-first century. The company also expected to increase its sales through derivatives, such as a light attack version, and by means of foreign military orders. It foresaw an international market of some 300 aircraft, and, not wanting to repeat its mistake with the A-10, it started promoting the product to potential foreign customers at a very early stage. The initial contract awarded to Republic was for the design, development, construction and testing of two prototypes and two static

test articles. Included in the fixed-price contract was an option for 54 production T-46As, representing the initial batch of the planned procurement which was to begin in 1984.

The T-46A was to be an efficient and economical solution to the multi-purpose jet trainer requirements of the 1980s and beyond. It was intended to replace the 35-year-old T-37 as the US Air Force's basic jet trainer and the AT-46A derivative, using the same airframe and engines, would fulfil the

Above left: To prove the T-46 design's outstanding flight characteristics, Republic flew this 62 per cent scale manned demonstrator before the contract was awarded. Piloted by Burt Rutan, the machine logged over 40hrs of flight time at Mojave, California, flying for over two months starting in September 1981.

Left: On 11 February 1985 the first of the expected 650 production T-46As was rolled out at Farmingdale. With new engines, new technology and new capabilities exceeding all the specifications, the Republic T-46 was to train more than 50,000 USAF pilots over the next 25 years. However, the roll-out proved to be a disaster for Republic and marked the beginning of the souring of relations with the Air Force.

Above: T-46A No. 1 on the ramp at Farmingdale. This well-designed aircraft was intended to be the efficient and economical solution to the problem of providing a multi-purpose jet trainer for the 1980s and beyond. The pronounced anhedral of the shoulder-mounted wing provided stability at high angles of attack and low air speeds, while the twin fins ensured that one unit was always in clear air while spinning, in order to facilitate a recovery.

additional role of weapons systems training. The key features of the T-46A included a top speed of more than 450mph, a quiet, pressurized cockpit, good, modern avionics and better manoeuvrability and an expanded flight envelope as compared to the T-37. The trainer's 425mph cruising speed would reduce the time needed to reach the practice area, allowing more actual time per mission, while its 47,000ft ceiling would permit much safer training because it could be performed above both the weather and the commercial traffic lanes. Side-by-side seating was incorporated for the best interaction between instructor and student pilot, the easy observation of mistakes made by a student allowing the instructor immediately to show him the correct procedure instead of having to attempt to describe it from the back seat over an intercom. The T-46 was equipped with two turbofan engines that offered high safety and permitted an easy transition to twin-engined advanced jet trainers or front-line fighters.

The T-46 wisely incorporated built-in design features so that it could easily be modified into an attack aircraft. Hardpoints for pylons were built into the wing, and with the simple addition of four underwing pylons, their associated stores management system and an optical sight or HUD the AT-46 could extend student pilot training into weapons delivery and attack; thus the basic design could be easily modified into a light attack

aircraft, much like the Cessna A-37, and it was this version that would, Republic felt, win it international sales. The AT-46A would have been able to carry two 500lb bombs, four 250lb bombs or two gun or rocket pods.

The T-46 was powered by two reliable, clean-burning, fuel-efficient Garrett F109 advanced turbofan engines each weighing only 400lb but producing 1,330lb of thrust. Features of the F109 included an immediate throttle response in all flight conditions, automatic ignition and starting, and a blow-out restarting capability. The engine was also provided with remarkably easy access, enabling it to be changed in 30min, and the twin-engined configuration would increase safety for the student and instructor, particularly at low altitudes.

In the design of the aircraft, the goals of high reliability and reduced maintenance requirements were considered as important as that of good performance and the result was a rugged, simple airframe with a guaranteed service life of 20,000hr – far more than any other trainer flying today; the Air Force expected to train some 50,000 pilots on the T-46 over its 25-year life. The airframe was mostly of riveted aluminium augmented by the selective use of composites (in general on the control surfaces and nose only) for ease of maintenance and repair. A simple, reliable flight control system consisting of protected cables and pulleys would keep maintenance

to a minimum and reduce the chances of malfunctions.

The T-46, which had a length of 29ft 6in, a wing span of 38ft 8in and a range of 1,400 miles, was a well thought out conventional design. It featured a cantiliver, light-alloy, two-piece wing, aero-dynamically a supercritical, low-drag design with a conventional two-spar box and stiffened skins. The fuselage was a semi-monocque, fail-safe structure of light alloy. The tail unit featured a cantilever, fixed-incidence tailplane with twin endplate fins and rudders (so that one rudder would always be in clear air while the aircraft was spinning, thereby facilitating recovery). The horizontal tail was clear of the wing wake at all times to ensure safe, predictable stalls.

Visually, the T-46 had a low nose stance for ease of cockpit access. The tricycle landing gear was hydraulically operated, the main units retracting inwards and forwards and the nose unit forwards. The two Garrett engines were mounted in nacelles beneath the wing roots. The shoulder-wing configuration ensured that wing stall would not introduce disturbed air into the inlet; furthermore, the deep-lipped engine inlets were located so that they did not obstruct cockpit entry. The T-46 also addressed a single-engine performance requirement, and the engine exhaust was deflected downwards to avoid impinging on the tail. The cockpit seated two persons side-by-side on McDonnell Douglas ACES II ejection seats equipped with canopy breakers in case the canopy failed to jettison. The pressurized and air-conditioned cockpit sat beneath a large clamshell canopy that opened upwards and rearwards, and the frameless windscreen was stressed to withstand a 4lb bird at 360kt. Only the aircraft's rudders were hydraulically boosted for assistance in spin recovery and crosswind landings, the other control surfaces being unboosted for simplicity of design and maintenance.

On 15 October 1985, the Fairchild-Republic T-46 trainer took to the air for a resoundingly successful maiden flight with Chief Pilot James Martinez at the controls. The aircraft reached

Above: One of the first four T-46s under construction. The structure was thoroughly conventional and the use of composite materials was kept to a minimum for ease of repair in the field.

an altitude of 15,000ft and a speed of 175kt during its planned 65-minute sortie. As Martinez commented after making a smooth touch-down, 'I've flown more than 100 different types of aircraft over the past twenty-four years and I don't think there's ever been one as easy to handle and forgiving as the T-46'.

Contractor Review

However, by 1985 engineering and manufacturing start-up costs on the T-46 had begun to rise alarmingly, necessitating the addition of $89 million in corporate reserves to 1984 added reserves of $11 million. These write-offs resulted from schedule slippages, engineering changes and unforeseen start-up costs; since Republic had a fixed-price contract, the company was forced to cover all costs above the contract limit.

Republic made its first major mistake on 11 February 1985 at the long-awaited roll-out of the first completed T-46. Fairchild-Republic and the Air Force had set the date two years earlier, and the company badly wanted to keep to it to prove its reliability and efficiency. A beautiful aircraft was indeed revealed at a large official ceremony, but Air Force staff discovered to their horror that it was by no means complete. It lacked some 1,200 internal components, and some skin sections were

Top: A T-46 tail section takes shape. The durable airframe was designed for 25 years of service. Only four T-46s rolled from Republic's assembly line, all others under construction being scrapped; the four survivors are still kept in sealed storage.
Above: The T-46 was powered by two durable, fuel-efficient Garrett F109 turbofan engines, tucked beneath the wing roots to present the minimum frontal area while providing easy access for removal.
Right: The T-46 incorporated a quiet, pressurized cockpit with side-by-side seating – an arrangement long recognized by the Air Force as the most efficient in ensuring co-ordination and observation between instructor and student.

Above: The second T-46 during its successful first flight from Republic Airport, 29 July 1986.

fabricated out of fibreglass and dummied up to look like finished sheet metal: frequent engineering changes and the late delivery of parts had set the company so far back that the only way it could roll out a 'completed' aircraft was to fake it. The discovery of this trickery marked the beginning of the souring of relations between the company and the Service. The débâcle of the missing parts left Air Force Secretary Aldridge so livid that he complained to Secretary of Defense Weinberger, who then ordered a rarely invoked contractor review.

The Air Force Contractor Review found deficiences in eight major aspects of the company's work, including manufacturing, engineering and product integrity. Many of the report's complaints were minor, such as poor food in the cafeteria and workers putting their lunches in a heat-treatment freezer. The company's prospects were not furthered by a fire in the engineering area, caused by a coffee pot being left plugged in over a weekend, which destroyed some of the original plans for the T-46. The report led to the Air Force suspending 50 per cent of the progress payments to Republic and to alleviate the problems Fairchild installed a new President, John Sandford, who made great efforts to overcome the manufacturing shortcomings.

In May 1986 the General Accounting Office issued a report saying that Republic had corrected most of its problems and that the T-46s had performed well in six months of flight tests at Edwards Air Force Base. The US

Congress appropriated funds for 33 T-46s in FY (Fiscal Year) 1986, and although the first production T-46 rolled off Republic's assembly lines in late 1986 the Air Force never released the money and it made no request for T-46s in FY87, mainly because of budgetary constraints: with the end of the Reagan era of high defence spending in sight, the Air Force decided that the T-46 was low on its list of priorities and could not be afforded. (When money is limited, the military inevitably prefers new weapons systems to new trainers.) Congress then cut $321 million from the Department of Defense Budget for T-46s in FY87, thus delivering a lethal blow to the project. The Air Force's only other primary jet trainers are Cessna T-37s, which date from the 1950s, yet it felt that it could get by with these aircraft until at least 1996, when another new trainer would be requested.

In 1986, after losing $167 million the previous year, the parent corporation, Fairchild, took drastic steps to stop the haemorrhage at Farmingdale. The SF-340 programme was terminated outright, Saab being left on its own to complete production. After first successfully addressing the issues arising from the Contractor Review in 1985, and then restoring the T-46 flight test programme to an acceptable level in 1986 (by now this involved three aircraft), the Air Force and Fairchild decided not to proceed with the project, both for purely financial reasons. In March 1987 Fairchild and the Air Force mutually agreed to

Above: The intended Air Force trainers for the 1980s: (from left to right) the Northrop T-38, the Cessna T-37 and the Republic T-46.

Right: In an attempt to expand sales of the T-46, Republic developed the AT-46 Full Spectrum Trainer. Also an armed export version aimed at the international market, the AT-46 would provide gunnery and light attack training in a fashion similar to the A-37. Republic reworked the original T-46 mock-up to include four underwing ordnance stations and a head-up display. Shown here, from left to right, are a triple ejector bomb rack, a General Electric SUU-11/A 7.62mm 'Gatling' gun pod; an FVV 0.50-calibre machine-gun and an LAU-68 2.75in folding-fin rocket pod. The demise of the T-46 also terminated this programme as well.

terminate the existing contract for the T-46 and all production work stopped immediately – literally during a coffee break.

All told, Fairchild lost $120 million on the T-46 programme. Four aircraft were built, and the Operational Readiness Evaluation, to be initiated by the 47th Flying Training Wing at Laughlin AFB, Texas, in the summer of 1987 with twenty aircraft, never took place. The three completed and delivered T-46s are currently in sealed storage at Davis-Monthan AFB, Arizona. Fairchild kept the fourth aircraft (P-2) and delivered it to their Voishon

subsidiary in California to use as a static test-bed for new fasteners, while the third and fourth production T-46s were destroyed at the Republic factory.

Finis

Since the SF-340 programme had ended and no new business was coming in, Fairchild felt it necessary to scale down operations at the Long Island plant in 1987 and dispose of it entirely in 1988: with the contraction in the military aircraft industry, and bearing in mind the expected limitations on new programmes,

Left: The end. With the closing of Republic, the last production workers file out of the desolate factory with their toolboxes, 12 October 1987. The view is of Building 17, the site of the assembly lines of so many historic aircraft. The last aircraft had already rolled out of The Thunder Factory.

Fairchild could see neither near- nor long-term opportunities for Republic as a military airframe builder. The remaining 3,500 employees were laid off as Fairchild decided to withdraw from aircraft production entirely. Without this production, Fairchild cut its losses to $8 million in 1986 and turned in a small profit for 1987. In 1988 the site of the Republic Aviation Corporation was sold, destined to become a shopping mall, and after 26,173 aircraft had been produced an era was over.

There were other, less obvious reasons why Republic failed – apart, that is, from the numerous managerial, tactical, political and engineering mistakes that so damaged the T-46. In October 1985 Fairchild Chairman Emanuel Fthenakis stood before a roomful of reporters at a Manhattan club and told them, in the midst of a Congressional fight to restore the T-46 programme, that Fairchild no longer wanted to be in the aircraft manufacturing business: Fairchild was clearly moving into the communications field and Fthenakis wanted to keep it that way. Once this attitude prevailed at the top, Republic was doomed. It also appears that Republic deliberately bid low to win the initial T-46 contract – the company was desperate for work in 1982. This is standard procedure in the industry (called 'low-balling'): you hope to win the contract and make money in the future. However, the

T-46's fixed-price contract left little money for development and start-up costs: over 100 aircraft would have had to be produced just to break even and the original contract was for only fifteen.

After the Air Force Contractor Review, Fairchild made no effort to secure additional work for Republic and Sandford's position was hopeless. John Sandford, the last President of Republic, travelled widely in the United States, trying to find a partner for the T-46, trying to secure additional work, trying to have the division bought outright by another major corporation, but Fairchild supported none of his efforts (made in his own time) and did not try to find new work for his company.

But finally, and most of all, Fairchild-Republic completely failed to diversify successfully out of the military aircraft market. In today's climate of defence budgets there is no way in which a company can survive solely as a military airframe manufacturer. Republic could survive only as long as it could keep at least one major aircraft contract going.

Sadly, after almost sixty years of building aircraft, the Republic Aviation Corporation no longer exists. However, its products still fly – every time an A-10 takes to the skies over Europe or the Space Shuttle is blasted into orbit. The pride and professionalism that created some of the greatest military aircraft of all time lives on.

Bibliography

Anderton, David. *Republic F-105 Thunderchief*. Osprey Publishing (London, 1983)

Chesneau, Roger. *Thunderbolt* II. Linewrights (Ongar, Essex, 1988)

Davis, Larry. *F-84 Thunderjet*. Squadron/Signal Publications (Carrollton, Texas, 1983)

Demaio, Robert. *A-10 Thunderbolt* II. Demaio (Lake Ronkonkoma, NY, 1981)

Drendel, Lou. *A-10 Warthog*. Squadron/Signal Publications (Carrollton, Texas, 1981)

Freeman, Roger. *Republic Thunderbolt*. Ducimus Books (London, 1977)

Freeman, Roger. *Thunderbolt*. (Charles Scribner's Sons (New York, 1979)

Hess William, *P-47 Thunderbolt at War*. Doubleday (Garden City, NY, 1977)

Johnson, Robert, and Caidin, Martin. *Thunderbolt!* Rinehart & Co. (New York, 1958)

Jones, Lloyd. *US Fighters*. Aero Publishers (Fallbrook, California, 1975)

Keaveney, Kevin. *Republic F-84 Swept-Wing Variants*. Aerofax (Arlington, Texas, 1987)

Kinzey, Bert. *F-105 Thunderchief*. Tab Books (Blue Ridge Summit, Pennsylvania, 1982)

Maloney, Edward. *Republic P-47 Thunderbolt*. Aero Publishers (Fallbrook, California, 1966)

Maloney, Edward. *Sever The Sky*. Planes of Fame (Corona Del Mar, California, 1979)

McDowell, Ernest. *Republic F/RF-84F Thunderstreak/Thunderflash*. Arco Publishing (New York, 1970)

Scutts, J. C. *F-105 Thunderchief*. Charles Scribner's Sons (New York, 1981)

Stafford, Gene. *Thunderbolt in Action*. Squadron/Signal Publications (Warren, Michigan, 1975)

Stoff, Joshua. *The Aerospace Heritage of Long Island*. Hofstra University (New York, 1989)

Waters, Andrew. *All the US Air Force Airplanes, 1907–1983*. Hippocrene Books (New York, 1983)

Index

Above: In 1938 a squadron of sleek P-35s clearly represented America's aerial might.

Below: This 1963 Republic design featured an 'aerospaceplane' with scramjet engines encircling the fuselage. Integrated engine and vehicle surfaces are still part of the current NASA scramjet spacecraft design.